"It's never too

The
Meaning
of
Health

the

Experience of a Lifetime

*An all-embracing, integrative picture of physical,
emotional, and spiritual well-being*

GARY ALLAN RATSON, MD

© Copyright 2003 Gary Allan Ratson. All rights reserved.

No part of this publication may be reproduced, stored in a retrieval system, or transmitted, in any form or by any means, electronic, mechanical, photocopying, recording, or otherwise, without the written prior permission of the author. Contact the author at the_souldoc@hotmail.com

Printed in Victoria, Canada

Editor: Patricia Anderson
Typography: Fiona Raven
Cover Photography: Virginia Fran
Cover Designer: Russ Davidson

```
National Library of Canada Cataloguing in Publication Data

Ratson, Gary Allan, 1960-
The meaning of health : the experience of a lifetime / Gary
Allan Ratson.Includes bibliographical references.
ISBN 1-4120-0228-1
1. Health--Philosophy.   I. Title.
R723.R38 2003          613'.01          C2003-902084-3
```

TRAFFORD

This book was published *on-demand* **in cooperation with Trafford Publishing.**
On-demand publishing is a unique process and service of making a book available for retail sale to the public taking advantage of on-demand manufacturing and Internet marketing.
On-demand publishing includes promotions, retail sales, manufacturing, order fulfilment, accounting and collecting royalties on behalf of the author.

Suite 6E, 2333 Government St., Victoria, B.C. V8T 4P4, CANADA
Phone   250-383-6864   Toll-free   1-888-232-4444 (Canada & US)
Fax   250-383-6804   E-mail   sales@trafford.com
Web site   www.trafford.com   TRAFFORD PUBLISHING IS A DIVISION OF TRAFFORD HOLDINGS LTD.
Trafford Catalogue #03-0597   www.trafford.com/robots/03-0597.html

10   9   8   7   6   5   4   3   2

"The Meaning of Health— the Experience of a Lifetime"

The Meaning of Health sees far beyond the mechanics of conventional and alternative health care. It values your decisions prior to your diagnosis and honors your perceptions long after your prognosis. It clearly points out that the purpose of facing unavoidable pain is to prevent needless suffering.

The Meaning of Health demands a higher context of all scientific, psychological, and spiritual evidence through deeper insights into your body, mind, and soul. Then, it excavates the remains of the ancient wisdom and scientific concepts that tend to get lost in the translation.

*Recognizing the inherent **purpose** in your own life assures you a sense of purpose in all of existence. This direct inner knowledge busts through the conflicting and confusing expert advice, making all problems and solutions a little more meaningful.*

*Feeling the unconditional **love** within your own nature affirms in you the benevolent support from all of nature. This mature inner love gives you a sense of belonging that lessens your longing, and looking for love in all the wrong places.*

*Taking **responsibility** for your own well-being gives you the courage to trust in your innate biological and spiritual healing. This internal strength eases the need for abusing any physical, financial, or authoritative power.*

*Recapturing your inner **freedom** releases your enslavement to neuroses, disabilities, and peer pressures, giving you hope for the possible and faith in the probable. This genuine joy also unlocks your sights from the limitations of others to freely see their solemn promise and sacred sovereignty.*

It is this living experience of purpose, love, responsibility, and freedom—at the levels of body, mind, and soul—that serves up an all-inclusive helping of health that forever satisfies. Of course, the meaning of good and evil, nature and nurture, and science and religion naturally come up when defusing the dispute over mind and matter. However, it is your evolving awareness that is most important for dealing with pain, lessening mistakes, and making all internal debate a little less daunting.

The endless search for the ultimate fix eases up, while the ceaseless struggle for absolute answers calms down, with the inner certainty that you knew all along. *The Meaning of Health* is written on many levels in a poetic style to induce your imagination wherever you happen to be. A deliberate read, with breaks for contemplation and discussion, helps the digestion of this soul food for thought.

"By sharing my childhood insights about purpose, love, responsibility, and freedom, I hope to prove that we all share an innate sense for healthy living, if needing only some context, consensus, and clarification."
— Gary Ratson

Acknowledgements

those who supported me and those who doubted
those who helped and those who hurt me
those who loved me and those who loathed me

ones who laughed with me and ones who laughed at me

people I've played with and played against
people I've admired and people I've abhorred
people I've helped and especially those I've hurt

for all the heroes and all the villains
you've all helped reveal the meaning

for

Lois and Nate Ratson

with love and gratitude

Table of Contents

Ideas of Health and.....
The Meaning of Health
    The Truth about the Truth
    The Meaning of Meaning
    It's a Question of Health
    The Stress of Life
    Can't Buy Me Love
    The Picture of Health

Instincts about Science and Spirit and.....
The Meaning of Science and Spirit
    Personality Plus
    Can We See Some ID?
    Conflicting Reports
    Meeting of Minds
    Four Dimensions of Health

Insights of Purpose and.....
The Meaning of Purpose
    The Nature of Purpose
    The Purpose of Nature
    Purpose at the Level of the Body
    Purpose at the Level of the Mind
    Purpose at the Level of the Soul
    The Will to Live
    Integrity and Character
    Values and Ethics

Imagining Love and.....
The Meaning of Love
- The Love of Nature
- The Nature of Love
- Love at the Level of the Body
- Love at the Level of the Mind
- Love at the Level of the Soul
- Loving Presence
- The Meaning of Children
- Lovin' Good Vibrations

Inferring Responsibility and.....
The Meaning of Responsibility
- The Nature of Responsibility
- The Responsibility of Nature
- Responsibility at the Level of the Body
- Responsibility at the Level of the Mind
- Responsibility at the Level of the Soul
- Aging and Death

Interpreting Freedom and.....
The Meaning of Freedom
- The Nature of Freedom
- The Freedom of Nature
- Freedom at the Level of Things
- Freedom at the Level of Thoughts
- The Free Spirit

Intuitions of Mind and.....
The Meaning of Mind
- The Physical Nature of Mind
- The Electric Nature of Mind
- The Soulful Nature of Mind
- Body, Mind, and Soul
- Is That All There Is?
- Soulful Savants
- Consciousness and Wisdom

Inclined to Believe and.....
The Meaning of Belief
 The Placebo Phenomenon
 The Nocebo Phenomenon
 The Nature of Nurture and
 The Nurture of Nature

Inventing a Lifestyle and.....
A Meaningful Life
 The Purpose of Food
 The Love of Food
 Responsible Eating
 The Purpose of Exercise
 The Love of Exercise
 Responsible Exercise
 Jog Your Memory

Beginning to see and.....
Beginning to Heal
 Contemplating Meditation

Suggested Reading

Ideas of Health

I never really became a doctor. I just took the course.

You see, I was more interested in the science than the system, more intrigued by the patient than the practice of medicine, and more concerned with experiencing health than building an identity as a physician. I had this vague and awkward notion that something about the patient was more vital to their overall well-being than all the experts and all the techniques designed to fix them.

For sure, the particular expression of symptoms, the unique degree of suffering, and the effectiveness of the treatment were beyond the reach of medical know-how. It was more critical and compelling for me to find some kernel of unchanging wisdom than to endlessly chase the latest test or treatment. Notwithstanding my squeamishness for invasive diagnostics and aggressive approaches, I had the inkling that there was more to health than met the eyepiece.

Early on in practice, I considered myself to be somewhat of a last resort. I developed a mutual attraction with patients who had already seen everyone, tried everything, or spent everything. For one thing, the serious diagnoses had been ruled out. Secondly, they were ready to listen to something new. My niche emerged by prescribing nothing and promising nothing. Without any annoying diagnosis or treatment to bother with, we were all finally forced to examine the meaning of pain and suffering.

My rebellious views of health grew increasingly embarrassing and even shameful. I wasn't getting with the medical program and this intellectual loneliness was predictive of an eventual isolation from colleagues. But misery loves company and I felt a strange certainty that whatever was missing in me was the same thing missing in patients, doctors, and the practice of medicine. I dug in there, but took no satisfaction in returning patients to lives I knew were contributing to their experience in illness.

Even by third-year medical school my misplaced expectations were painfully obvious. Asking my instructors and advisors if their decade-long patients were any healthier was nonsense to them. But innocently enough, I wanted to be ten years healthier in ten years. I didn't think it was naive to put a dent in the direction of people's lives. If only I could put a dent in the direction of my own.

To the extent I grew up, you might say I had everything. With enough food, clothing, and opportunity, even I thought all this internal strife was rather odd. With a caring family and no serious upsets, I was embarrassed and ashamed to feel so embarrassed and ashamed about my life.

But who else better to whine about the subtle conflicts and confusions than someone who has no other pressing issues? I didn't need everything—I needed something else. I needed to know what the hell I was doing. Doing what I was told wasn't going to cut it. I had no idea what I wanted to do or how to decide; I just knew that I wanted to understand it and that I needed to love it. It was an emotional urge more than any intellectual search for meaning. Thank God those adults knew what they were doing....

Without major childhood trauma, I appeared fairly normal and well-adjusted in my relationships with friends, in school, and in sports. I hung out in the park, filled in the blanks, and open-field tackled as well as anyone. It wasn't that difficult to follow the crowd, follow directions, and follow the leader. I wasn't a complete idiot.

Any accolades, achievements, and awards that I was able to score did little to ease the certainty that I was faking it big-time. I didn't have a clue and began dragging my feet as I walked through the motions. For all intents and purposes, I assumed I was lazy. Dad called it contempt. It was unavoidable that I would waste whatever talents I had and miss whatever opportunities presented, waiting for time and age to bring me some kind of wisdom.

"Don't worry," everyone said, "You're doing fine, everyone feels like that." Yeah, right. Parents, teachers, and coaches were all losing my confidence fast. They couldn't quite hear me when I said, "No, I'm not fine." My best hope, my educated guess, was that education was the only way out. Surely professors, scientists, and psychologists knew what they were talking about....

I had somewhat alternative reasons for entering medical school in the first place. Others said they wanted to help people. That seemed as obvious to me as it was simplistic. I thought that if I knew how to live a healthy life, maybe I could teach someone else. Surely a medical education would open doors and provide lots of options. Plus, I had nothing else to do. I slipped into med school on a low tide—the lowest average admission scores in history or something like that.

So anyway, two years later I was in the Dean's office. I was sent down for a quick mental health check before a year off for good behavior. In truth, I needed a respite from total misery, apathy, and dishonor. "Listen, son, I didn't have any idea what I was doing for the first ten years of practice." (*You see, this is what I was trying to avoid.*) Then it came. "But you're doing fine, really. Everyone feels like that." *Arrrgghhhh. Actually, I just smiled while crying to myself.*

But I went back nine months later, refreshed, renewed, and regardless. I might as well take the knowledge and run, file the prestige for what it's worth, and hope for the best. My tantrum continued only slightly disguised as aloofness and indifference. I tried to deny my anger at the system and its colluding patients for letting me down.

Over the next many years, anger turned inward toward despair and felt like disgrace. I refused to accept what surprised me as an enormous power and influence over people's lives. I was no authority on health—at least not the kind of health I wanted to experience.

In time, I found great solace in books. I studied more, and with more satisfaction, than I ever did in school. And I meant it. I feverishly filled in the gaps in my formal education with what I needed most. From the strictest science to the most esoteric scriptures, it was all one subject to me—the subject of health. I didn't need to become proficient at anything—I just wanted to get the idea of everything.

Most alternative medicine is recently translated and often distorted from the ancient healing and mystic traditions. Hypnosis, acupuncture, meditation, yoga, and the rest all have something important to say about health. But again, I wasn't interested in selling and promoting more stuff. I wanted to know what the wisdom behind these enduring disciplines meant for everyday life.

As I pieced together a bigger picture of health, I felt the puzzle of my own jumbled life fall into place—somewhat. School was finally in. Authors' words spoke to me as if we were in the same room, conversing like best friends. Other humanoids had had similar experiences, asked similar questions, and expressed them beautifully. Maybe just maybe, I wasn't merely a lazy malcontent.

The impact of my research was so moving and hopeful that for the first time I knew it was possible that ideas could change lives. I fell in love with books and the people who wrote them. Writing seemed to me just about the best thing anyone could do. Sure, there are many more average books than brilliant ones, but someone summoned the courage to put their thoughts out there. For me, it was the beginning of a faraway dream, one full of fears, doubts, and uncertainties.

Still, it was no near-death experience and old habits die hard. Reading became a curious addiction. Getting the same confirming messages over and over wasn't enough to stop living vicariously through my creative heroes. It's all been said before, there's nothing new under the sun, and I'm not going to say it any better than these guys. Without the heartfelt passion and the steadfast commitment, I was just another "ass with a load of books" (and a whole lot of excuses).

I could think outside the box, I just couldn't crawl out of it. Friends and family were as supportive as they could be without really knowing what I was talking about. The best they could offer was, "You're thinking too much, you're living inside your head, and you're not living your life." They were partially right, but you're supposed to think.

Seeing many authors speak in person, it occurred to me that they benefited the most from the experience. I mean, by saying it a thousand different ways, a thousand different times, in response to a thousand different questions, the speaker relearns it, reinvents it, and relives it. Animated, passionate, and committed, the writers actually live what often seems like idealistic rhetoric to the poor saps in the audience. Plus, everyone seems to think the speaker is pretty hot stuff. At best, the viewing public might enjoy the evening out and remember one or two pearls.

To become my own expert, write my own ticket, and live my own life—wow—that's the only way to go. Not even as a professional necessarily, but in an ordinary way of trusting my instincts, writing my destiny, and creating my own fun. I still needed a ton of assurance, but I was inspired enough to think I might have something to offer. It was the first time I knew for sure that I couldn't be the only idiot out there with these backward ideas.

With all this free time, maybe I could turn my middle class angst, education, and luxuries into an authentic life that honored those writers who've saved me while maintaining a degree of social conscience. My idea of a healthy life and career was an ideal of expressing what was in my soul with all my heart. I would use the experience to inspire others rather than merely catching them when they fall.

After years of not doing anything, there was nothing left for me 'not' to do. As it turned out, I still let the pain of not doing anything become greater than the fear of finally putting something down before I began to write. It didn't *take much courage to take the road less traveled when it was the path of least resistance. By this time, I really had nothing to lose. Everyone already thought I was more than a little bit crazy, eccentric, or paranoid. That was quite liberating, actually. Maybe I was slowly becoming a writer—on paper anyway.*

This book seemed bent on writing itself. I didn't channel it or anything like that, but it did take on a mind of its own. Although, when a book writes itself, and I looked in on it from time to time, nothing much gets done. As resistant, scared, and timid as I was about writing for public consumption, a book did gradually appear. The chapters seemed to emerge all at once rather than one at a time. They all got clearer, first as the stanzas of a poem, then as the sessions of a seminar, and then very leisurely into this paper weight. If it rings a bell with one poor soul, I'll consider it a miracle.

The Meaning of Health

*Everything can be expressed in words
except the living truth.*
— Mircea Eliade

The chances of finding the meaning of health in the dictionary are as likely as discovering the meaning of life in the encyclopaedia. While the descriptions give us some agreements for everyday communication, they are a million miles away from explaining what health really looks like. Everyone wants to live a healthy life. But until we grasp the depths of what health really feels like, we're just scratching the surface.

The essence of human experience has always been difficult to put into words. Definitions act to define the borders and delineate the limits that convey isolated concepts. Meaning, on the other hand, blows holes in old notions and integrates idle ideas, in attempts to capture the lived experience. Now, a picture may well paint a thousand words, but a clear and concise picture of health requires a perceptual skill long after the books have been thoroughly digested. Yet, the image may seem strangely familiar.

The meaning of health doesn't even make any sense, scientifically. Medical science is concerned with measuring disease mechanisms and dispensing with the debate about meaning. But note the glitch between the objective rock of scientific scrutiny and the hardhead of the subjective patient. The object of inquiry here happens to be a subject—a subject that likes to know the meaning of things, lest it get cranky and noncompliant. The science of medicine runs smack into the conflict between facts and values, while the art of medicine tries to keep the meaning of both in mind.

That is why, in this artful discussion about meaning, we're allowed the luxury and the challenge of suggesting that the meaning of health is not purely an intellectual pursuit. We can get that anywhere. Released from the rigid rules of impartial evidence, we are limited only by our imagination and intuition, while still yielding to logic, reason and consensus. Of course, this just happens to be the origin of any and all scientific hypothesis.

If the meaning of health seems redundant at best and neurotic at worst, let's remember all the superfluous terms that we've found to take up the slack. While expressing a need that is not generally satisfied by medicine, the current buzzwords like "*holistic,*" "*natural,*" "*wellness,*" and "*wholeness*" reflect the missed meaning of the original term. These popular adjectives suggest that the word "*health*" itself has been, admittedly, doctored. Yet, the hectic health care system needs the push from these New Age adjectives to enliven, if not exaggerate, the long forgotten and ignored ideals of real health.

Poor old health has suffered the fate of any well meaning cliché. Once vibrant and forceful, full of power and promise, health has been misused, misunderstood, and misappropriated. Health has become a commodity, reduced to types of health care—the things other people sell, deliver, and do to us. Conventional, alternative, and complementary medicine all refer to different philosophical approaches to diagnosis and treatment of symptoms. The personal experience of health lives before and after these clinics ever opened or closed for the weekend.

Like love or spirituality, a coherent discussion about health demands serious study about its meaning. Beyond mere philosophical psychobabble and New Age rhetoric, the cultural consensus of health underlies the actual practice of treating patients, teaching students, and raising children. It's this same mutual meaning of health that silently directs the focus and funding of our research, public policy, and laws.

Science and technology have yielded an impressive mastery over things. All our iron-fisted machinery though, remains less impressive for living things and even less masterful over thinking things. High-tech toys are easy distractions from the part of life that stainless steel can't cut and computers can't calculate—the human part.

All of our incredible modern advances leave one wondering about all the persistent human suffering. There's more than enough money, food, and communications to stem the starvation, poverty, and conflicts around the world. But the subtle underpinnings of human hardship are more than elusive for the heavy hammers of modern technology. The state of the world's health reflects the state of the world's minds—and their understanding of health.

Addictions, divorce, and chronic pain are some of the personal problems not amenable to the quick medicinal fix. What we make of our situation figures strongly in our response to any management or treatment. We can wait for Gene Therapy Drive-Thru's and Artificial Intelligence Cafes to heal our lives or we can examine the meaning of the trouble spots, right now. Cultural values and societal wisdom have never kept pace with intellectual achievements. But individually, it's easy to be years ahead of our time, if we want to be.

The definitions of health do continue to expand, slowly but surely, with the march of scientific knowledge. The widening scope of health care and medical research reflects the public perception of what is in society's best interests. But these growing concerns of health always originate from a deeper appreciation of its meaning, which in turn comes from personal experience. Conversely, by refusing to examine the tired old meaning of health, we undermine the natural creation of better definitions.

Dorland's Medical Dictionary defines health as "*a state of optimal physical, mental, and social well-being, not merely the absence of disease.*" That sounds pretty good. But the working definition of health in chaotic teaching hospitals is more likely to read *minimal* than *optimal*—not usually the best places for a meaningful healing experience. Medical treatment in hospitals is like rehabilitation in prison—there's a high rate of recidivism.

The current World Health Organization's definition goes a giant step further by suggesting that health is "*The extent to which an individual or group is able to raise aspirations and satisfy needs, and to change or cope with the environment. It is a resource for everyday life, not the object of living; it is a positive concept emphasizing social and personal resources, as well as physical, mental, and spiritual capacities.*" That's quite an impressive and inclusive little snapshot. But even the WHO cannot live up to this ideal unless they live it on a daily basis.

First, health needs to be deeply understood. Then it needs to be truly experienced and accepted by the majority before it's incorporated into a working system of values and practices. Hectic surgical suites and exhausting medical practices, without the time or resources, cannot possibly live up to these ideals. But we can.

Words and concepts, like science and technology, work better for describing things than they do for explaining our experience of things. Our definition of health is further limited by our definition of life, which mysteriously enough, defies definition. Dorland's again states that life is *"an aggregate of vital phenomena; a certain peculiar stimulated condition of organized matter; that obscure principle whereby organized beings are peculiarly endowed with certain powers and functions not associated with inorganic matter."*

It would seem that the total well-being of a *"peculiar stimulated condition"* is going to present somewhat more than a challenge. While our slowly evolving views of life and health have begun to include matter, mind, and spirit, none of these terms are very definitive either. To arrive at any practical understanding of a healthy life, the meaning of health obliges us to consider our own experience of biological, psychological, and spiritual realities.

Physicists probe the depths of lowly matter. Rather than fundamental structural units, the solid sensation of molecules is sustained by ill-defined energy processes. These are largely known by mathematical probabilities and theoretical possibilities. While the energetic and quirky characteristics can be exploited for microtechnology, the relevance to biological health remains cloudy. Even the origin of the material universe in the Big Bang Theory remains murky and fudged a bit to account for the first few minutes.

Yet the nuts and bolts of all things, both living and dead, are made up of the same eerie subatomic bits and pieces, varying only in quantity and arrangement. To understand the nature of ourselves, we need to get a feel for the crux of this subtle matter.

Biology describes incredibly complex cellular and molecular processes. Yet strangely enough, biologists are forced to ignore the actual life force that energizes them. There is no physics to account for the animating power and vitality of growth, repair, and healing mechanics. Science is also at a loss to explain the origin of life—that little matter of the material world inducing itself to wake up and smell the coffee.

The mundane stuff of rocks and stars mysteriously organized itself with the ability to eat, think, and complain. None of this is even relevant for the business of health care. But since we share the same biological origins and cellular language with the rest of the species, it behooves us to consider of the nature and origin of life if we want to better understand the meaning of health.

The sheer number of psychological therapies show the lack of consensus on the precise nature of the mind and its symptoms. Current trends lean toward a biopsychology, as the brain is somewhat easier to probe than the mind. But experiments with the brain are not synonymous with the experience of the mind.

The mind is defined as "*the faculty of the brain that allows awareness of surroundings, as well as experience of emotions, reason, and memory.*" It's funny that the faculty of medicine remains oddly inattentive to the very emotional, reasonable, and memorable circumstances that sanction its very existence. By definition, science and medicine are forced to favor the matter of the body over the mind.

Still, our perception of illness significantly affects the degree of our suffering and the aggressiveness of our response. Contemplating the origin of our own thoughts is vital to realizing the subjective influences on the source and severity of all symptoms.

Now, the soul doesn't quite make the medical dictionary and spirit only shows up as "*the volatility of a distilled liquid.*" Any animating intelligence, however defined, will remain a private encounter within our awareness. Theology, religion, and mysticism will continue to explore, interpret, and teach the ancient scriptures and oral traditions, but any certainty as to the genesis or integrity of the precepts is left to our personal consideration.

We're left then, with the most perilous gap in our understanding of health. As long as the mind is immeasurable and the soul is immaterial for medical science, any mutual influence between body, mind, and soul are precipitously perched at the flakey edge of pseudo science. This makes any mind-body-soul debate irrelevant to scientific discussion or at best reduces it to a brain-body dialogue. Any intuitive certainty of health again relies on our own organic sureness, based on familiarity, education, and *not-so-common*, common sense.

But we already know more than we realize. Biased, fragmented, and hugely diverse disciplines make it difficult to take advantage of all available information. The information we do use is less useful as patents, profits, and political motives oust it from its rightful context. It's easier to keep groping for more and more facts, than ponder the value of knowledge already at hand.

You see, the meaning of objective evidence is always at the mercy of someone's interpretation. Refining our subjective sphere of knowing is itself a type of healing for which medics can only imagine. Importantly, this growing wisdom eventually allows us to utilize any treatment and technology wisely.

The closest we can get to the ultimate realities, out there, is by fearlessly confronting the intimacy of the physical, emotional, and spiritual mysteries, in here. Then, by comparing and confirming with others we become our own modern day mystic—with access to computers and communications.

The Truth about the Truth

> *The best we can do is use all available knowledge to encircle the truth.*
> — Viktor Frankl

Truths are like lies—we keep getting caught in them. Any truth to the meaning of health will prove itself to be self-evident and internally consistent. As a subjective truth, there is no convincing or arm twisting required. The truth of health just keeps popping up.

The word "*health*" is derived from "*wholeness,*" which prompts one to consider the meaning of the word "*whole.*" To the extent that *our* truth about health applies to the well-being of families, culture, and the environment as well as the state of business, government, and education, it's a *whole* truth. When health actually *means* health, everything's included.

The living truth, as it is, is no further than our own living experience. Our perception of everything else is limited to this experiential truth. The meaning of health honors this truth without defining, capturing, or corrupting it. It points toward something more terrific than our troubles, more authentic than our therapy, and far more profound than the packaging, sales, and statistics of modern health care.

The truth about health is revealed by how honestly we face up to all our experiences. This sincere vision then allows us to revisit all the scientific and spiritual evidence in a productive and meaningful manner. Still, nothing is more certain and substantial than trusting our own hard-won awareness of the situation.

The Meaning of Meaning

> *It's better to read one book a thousand times than to read a thousand books.*
> — Buddhist Aphorism

The ancient Hindu scriptures refer to reality as "*Not this, not that.*" The Taoist Lao Tzu holds that "*If you can say it, it's not the Tao,*" while one Buddhist suggests that "*If you see Buddha walking down the street, kill him.*"

The point is that it's easier to say what the meaning of health is *not*. The meaning of health is not a new concept, philosophy, or treatment modality. It has no bottom line, no elevator synopsis, and no abridged notes. The ultimate nature of anything ultimately defies our descriptions. Like real life, having a good eye for health means we have to show up and see for ourselves.

We can all readily admit to knowing more about nutrition, fitness, and relationships than we care to incorporate into daily life. Endless details hardly guarantee a change in motivation or behavior. Even a college education impresses its graduates more through socialization and learning skills than by highfalutin and forgotten facts. Similarly, the common fear tactics with disease statistics are not enough to modify the manner of the masses. Only when new meaning forces us to see things differently do we spontaneously begin to change our wandering ways.

How many books do we have to read? How many diets, fitness programs, seminars, and techniques do we have to try before we realize that the dent in our bookshelf and our bank account is bigger than in the direction of our life?

We've been getting endless advice, analysis, and admonishments from everyone everywhere since we were born. The so-called self-help movement sells more books, tapes, and courses than it engenders genuine transformations. How much can we really get from an instructional book unless it's moving enough to shove us over the edge? That emotional push is often missing in expert opinion and professional advice. Just notice who has all the weight loss, get-rich-quick, and relationship-rescue books. To be sure, it's not the presumed slim, rich, and happy couples.

You see, the ten steps to success, the seven principles of life, and the six weeks to health are not actual steps, principles, or weeks—someone just made them up. The authors' experiences may well have been real, but their written words and concepts are a symbolic guide, a reminder, or even a metaphor. The strongest voice and the most healing effects are in the unspoken message between the lines of a truly creative effort.

The meaning of health cannot be bound by the covers of another *How-to* book. If anything, this "Meaning of Health" is a coloring book or a messy finger painting of our own glorious self-portrait. Let's start a trend with the first and foremost *Why-to* or *Why-bother* book.

Think about the origin of all the instructional guides for our favorite sports. The top athletes sit down to explain just how it's done. They break it down to the fundamentals of training, strategies of competition, and mental toughness techniques—hopefully there's an inspiring personal struggle. But even with a careful dissection, it's difficult for them to impart just exactly how they do it. The journeymen players, like losing coaches, have all mastered the same fundamentals, strategies, and techniques. Even with the most sincere motivation, inspiration, and perspiration, no one can give us what we need most.

The same star athletes weren't the ones reading books back in the day. They were out in the backyard making miracles happen. Physical gifts, talents, and the fortune to indulge them; passion, creativity, and the courage to live them; genius, competitive spirit, and the chutzpah to express them—these impulses all emerged and were sustained by the *meaning* that the sport held for them. We have to experience that for ourselves. When we fall in love with the way our heroes fell in love with what they do, then our own dreams and creativity will be our most trusted guides.

That's how successful people really do it. Socrates said, "*Wisdom cannot be taught, but only known directly."* Motivated by love, the great athletes carve out their own style. Like poetry in motion, they gracefully became their own best teacher and trusted coach. Hey, maybe then we could write a book about how we did it or better yet, why we bothered.

Manuals work better for repairing cars. Life's biggest lessons happen *to* us. Cultivating moving experiences, meeting memorable people, and nurturing creative insights all serve to remind us of something meaningful about health that we left in our toy box. Ceaseless searching for answers is a constant distraction from the reflection and insight that leads to a better class of questions.

It's a Question of Health

> *Doubt may be an uncomfortable condition,*
> *but certainty is a ridiculous one.*
> — Voltaire

Questions are to answers as meaning is to definitions. Questions set the tone and determine the limits of the answers. Silence at the end of a lecture assures the professor that nobody has a clue. Questions are signs of understanding. Just as definitions expand as meaning heightens, so solutions endure as long as the inquiry is deep.

The quick fixes, miracle cures, and promised panaceas that come and go in popular culture are the passing answers to shallow questions. The meaning of open-ended curiosity and persistent intrigue are far more healing in the long run than the mechanics of short-term salves, single saves, and magic bullets.

Like any good theory, tonics and remedies are only useful until a better one comes along. But in our desperation and anticipation for anything *new and improved,* we often bypass the best interests of immediate health and long-term happiness. The meaning of health champions the patient's perceptions over their prescriptions, the healing process over the prognosis, and the person's experience over the promise of the experimental treatment. The meaning of health begs for a bigger and better questioning process than merely the myriad of questionable products.

Missing Persons

> *It's more important to know what sort of person has the disease than what sort of disease has the person.*
> — Sir William Osler, MD

Medicine has generally declared its mandate somewhere between *"Come back if it gets worse"* and *"I'm sorry, but there's nothing we can do."* Medicine means to measure, and the more positive results on tests, x-rays, and blood work, then the greater the possibility for diagnosis and treatment. Yet years before anything shows up on x-ray and years after they pronounce us incurable, our experience of ill-health is happening right now, between office visits—24/7. A disease or dysfunction doesn't just pop into existence the day we finally get in for an MRI scan. The apparent incidence of any disease is always limited by this ability to measure.

Modern medicine has advanced to the point where doctors can virtually ignore us and still do a pretty good job. Watch out for telenet-surgery. Space-shuttling technologies seem more miraculous than the phenomenal boy wonders that dream up these things. The person in all its glory is so matter of fact, so work-a-day dull, as to be beside the point. Value-free scientific facts are valued more than the people who determine their value and then pretend that they're value-free. By coveting our creations more than our creativeness, we diminish even the mechanical advantage of medical treatment.

Many people experience this alienation from medicine and turn to the often more artful alternative practitioners. Still, the focus tends to be on external potions, procedures, and procurements that further distract from personal responsibilities and vital needs. The meaning of treatment is tied to just how and why it's concocted, counseled, and consumed. And the meaning of treatment naturally forces us to examine the meaning of symptoms.

Medicine can't speak of a healing force and doesn't pretend to enliven it. Spontaneous growth, repair, and renewal curiously fly in the face of the objective intentions of medical science. Like the original spark of life, biological healing represents the still smoldering embers that can't be controlled or patented and, at best, remains a peripheral entity in conventional medicine.

The Hippocratic Oath implores doctors to *"Firstly, Do No Harm."* But the meaning of *"harm"* changes with varying views of health. The history of medicine is the history of well intended, yet harmful side effects, excessive measures, and barbaric practices. The harm became more and more subtle and indirect as modern treatment grew more sophisticated. Today, it is the inadvertent withholding, denying, or forgetting what the patients, children, and citizens need most that inflicts the most harm.

There is no importance given to psychological modeling of health in medicine. We would no doubt be leery about a slovenly nutritionist, a sloppy aerobics instructor, or a slouchy yoga teacher. Like coaches, teachers, and parents, these practitioners influence us greatly by their example. But the harder a discipline defines itself to be, the less weight is given to such soft suggestion.

Doctors are not any healthier than anyone else in their socio-economic group. This is neither contrary nor necessary to their ideas of health and doesn't even mean anything to them. Cookbook medicine as the technical servicing of human pumps, pipes, and plumbing is reasonable enough. But prescribing treatment wisely requires the wisdom of the healer's own healing experience. The disease orientation of modern medicine creates the contradiction within the medical misnomer—*health care.*

The façade of the doctor's white coat, oak desk, and authoritative air help to maintain some distance, objectivity, and power. After all, physicians can't personally take on the suffering of every patient all day long. Yet this detachment and denial paradoxically results in an accumulation of subconscious stress leading to one of the highest professional rates of addiction, divorce, and suicide. Doctors are people too, and no amount of scary statistics is enough for them to change their ways, anymore than fear-mongering for deadly disease is sufficient for us to change ours.

Chronic fatigue and pain syndromes, irritable bowel—like low back pain and the rest—beg doctors to look at the person because there's nothing else to see. The tests are often normal, the x-rays are clear, and the blood work is fine. Without much to measure, these syndromes don't really exist—medically speaking.

One might think that without any pesky details to get in the way, it should be a no-brainer that something about the person affects the cause, the cruelty, and the course of their illness. Patients and doctors alike lack the mind-set to recognize what they all know in their hearts to be true—that their dis-ease is due, in part, to their strained view of the world.

Only after years of repetitive reporting are patients with chronic symptoms begrudgingly granted a label, if only a syndrome—a collection of symptoms of unknown origin. There's still nothing to treat, but for the time being they don't feel so foolish. The condition doesn't get an actual name until there is objective proof that it ever existed—in the lab.

Happy to be honored with even a syndrome, sufferers now have the acknowledgment that they're not crazy, their pain is not all in their heads, and others indeed share the same experience. Eventually though, that small achievement wanes as they are forced to create their own support groups and sympathy networks. They're surviving, but not really healing. When an illness is meaningless, the treatment is a close second, and the patient is third.

The same process is seen globally as humanitarian groups set up huge humanitarian efforts. These are the support groups for worldwide syndromes of poverty, hunger, and conflict of no known cause. The meaning of this global suffering also slips through the cracks in the will of powerful governments—also made up of individuals, the last time anyone checked.

Medicine is a product of the culture, and so health care shares in the same deficiencies as all institutions. Personal perceptions, like worldwide perspectives, are too soft for health care dollars, too smart for bombs, and too tenuous for technology. The meaning of health considers the meaning of suffering vital for any legitimate health care. So the fix is in. The meaning of health is about examining our lives, no matter how stressful.

The Stress of Life

> *Science ignores experience when doing science and we ignore science when leading life.*
> — Francis Varela

Dr. Hans Selye was ahead of his time when he pondered the common feature he noticed in all his patients—they all looked sick. Considered the father of stress medicine, Dr. Selye went on to elucidate the biochemistry behind the faces of stressful circumstances. He detailed the short and long-term hormonal, immune, and central nervous system responses to real and perceived danger.

Of course this is the flight or fight response, the Biology 101 survival mechanism that provides the quick energy for life threatening situations. By piercing the specific symptoms, Dr. Selye could hear the echoing angst beneath the patient's digital readout. He was asking bigger questions.

Yet the *meaning* of stress still gets left in the halls of the health care system, along with the stressed out people. Conventional medicine can't pin the origins of disease on the mechanisms of stress. Stomach ulcers were definitely caused by stress, until an acid-loving bacterium came along to take the blame—and the punishment. And now, as we search for bacteria to target for every disease, we might wonder if the little critters didn't live in enteric harmony during the weeks and months leading up to an emotional incite to riot—and *then* torched the hole in the stomach lining.

With stress chemistry known to hinder immunity, maintenance, and healing in general, researchers still require a singular molecular mechanism to unlock a specific disease with the smartest key. As long as disease is deemed a specific end product and stress remains a continuous process, then never the two shall meet. Of course, many medications are still used without a precisely known mechanism—part of the humor and hypocrisy in medicine.

We all know what we mean by stress. It weighs on the pillars of our physiology. But even upset sleep, menstruation, digestion, and elimination are not taken as serious medical concerns. Everyone knows that stress makes their existing pain worse and hinders the response to treatment, while making the ability to cope much more of a challenge. Only after years of easing this stress with excessive drinking, smoking, gambling, or just plain wallowing in it, might the documented aftermath finally be covered by our current medical plan.

We've all experienced blushing, palpitations, dry mouth, and sweaty palms. Many people have lost their breath, frozen in motion, or feebly fainted in an anxious or panicky attack, none of which specifically causes disease. But these awkward moments make it easier to imagine how mental rigidity can sway our body's resilience.

Still, ruling out stress as part of the puzzle is as much of a mistake as force-fitting stress as the single cause of any dysfunction. It's this either/or view that creates much of the stress that we're still forced to live with. As a mere nuisance, it's best left for the gym, the spa, or the pharmacy.

Without the need for medical attention, it's up to us to spell relief. Our first stop is that over-the-counter buffet—that cornucopia of pharmacopoeia—our neighborhood drugstore. It's easy enough to suppress the minor annoyances, relieve any irritations, and dull the memory completely to get on with more important things. At least it's convenient to stock up on snacks, smokes, and spirits while we wait for our sleeping pills, suppositories, and SpaceTabs. When we relieve our stress by indulging our vices, the pharmacist can survive another day to attend to the smaller but inevitable business of our eventual disease care.

Hey, there's no evidence to suggest that thirty years of smothering, resisting, and ignoring these little bumps and bruises leads to anything serious. Except that thirty years of constipation, indigestion, insomnia, and anxiety are a serious chunk of life. And we can be certain to find one or all of these so-called "*associated*" features in all chronic conditions.

The casual overuse of antidepressants and multiple misuses of sedatives drive the final nail in the coffin of any meaning for life's ups and downs. And the widespread abuse of happy-pills and attention-getters show our contempt for any biological intelligence.

In truth, the stress response is not something to suppress, but something to express. It's a living dimmer switch for business-as-usual rather than an on-off mechanism for momentary special effects.

Imagine a dynamic continuum of metabolism where one end is a calm, peaceful state for growth and healing—the relaxation-response. The other end is an excited, war-time, energy-depleting state—the better known stress-response. Our perception of imminent danger is the toggle that dials in where we live along the continuum and just how deeply we fall into harm's way.

It's not even our stress level per se that is particularly bad. We can be scared to death as much as bored to death. Both high and low stress is eventually harmful. To be sure, there are subtle biochemical nuances beyond our understanding and equipment. But the *quality* of the stress is as important as the *quantity*. Even happy or sad tears have a slightly different biochemistry. The body knows whether we're running scared or invigorated by the fight, whether our excitement is fueled by fear or by love. The raw special effects of passion are wonderfully real but the scary side effects are often left to our frightful imagination.

We now have the luxury of calmly and reasonably salvaging the meaning of the good doctor's discoveries about stress. Peering deeper yet into people's eyes, we can see past the facial features and physical chemistry into their hearts and minds. Beyond their defensive postures, sluggish movements, and troubled expressions we might just detect a sagging will.

Beyond the continuum of obvious stress, we might notice a deeper, underlying continuum—one of a subtle spiritual strain that creates and sustains much of the physical peril. This spiritual vacuum would surely constrict intelligent reactions to problems, draw out senseless suffering, and basically, suck the soul out of life. The meaning of health must embrace a sophisticated meaning of spiritual well-being.

Human greed, consumption, and conflict are really the desperate attempts to fill this hole-in-our-heart to one degree or another. Deep rooted hopelessness, powerlessness, and loneliness inform many needless aches and pains—the flashing vacancy signs for faith, strength, and belonging.

Largely beyond the scope of medical intervention, these spiritual epidemics oblige us to unearth their meaning for ourselves. Otherwise, they continue to foster the behaviors and responses that make things worse. Even talk therapy is often at a loss to seal this void in the human soul. If stress management doesn't address the origin and meaning of stress, it's just another car manual.

Intelligent doctors who used to smoke cigarettes must have deemed their coughing, wheezing, and shortness of breath to be harmless enough, until the statistical discomfort became too hard to ignore. Today, nobody can afford to ignore their hearts and minds while waiting for science to heal their lives.

We're up against a culture that insists, *"You're fine, it's not your fault. Life is unfair."* But a faint chorus sings back from enlightened souls that admit, *"Life is truly a lot more beautiful than it appears, but your view finder is smudged."* It sounds like a lifelong challenge of facing painful issues ad infinitum—but there it is. Oh yeah, this kind of soulful healing also promises the most joy in life, if we have the time.

Of course, managing stress would be a lot easier if there was less of it. Most stress is unnecessary. There aren't too many saber-toothed tigers running around the neighborhood these days and the primitive stress response has been crying wolf much too often. All illness is aggravated by fear and anxiety and most doctor visits have an added component of dread and despair.

Imagine the relief to the health care system if hospitals were free to focus on the obvious and urgent disasters. Shortages of hospital beds, money, and technology would be a thing of the past if the system were freed from overwhelming preventable problems. Envision our own leisure to maneuver life's inexplicable incidents, injuries, and calamities with the time and energy we've spared from the silly stuff.

While physicists search for a unified theory of everything, we can begin a unified approach to everything that hurts. Common physical ills like high blood pressure, heart disease, and stroke share narrow and resistive arteries. Common functional and chronic psychosomatic symptoms often reveal a reduced blood flow and restricted movements. And common emotional conflicts share narrow and rigid views of nature and human nature.

Now common things being common, excessively inflamed tissues and emotions, exaggerated rigidity of muscles and mind-sets, and needlessly stressed bodies and minds, are more than sophomoric metaphors. A world of helplessness, fearfulness, and meaninglessness has created the pandemic pandemonium that screams for the kind of relief that only comes from the inside out.

The spiritual sensibility that is missing in our stressed-out society suggests a unified source of healing. It's this inner wealth that affords us the caring, coping, and reconciling skills for the unavoidable, untreatable, or incurable ills—a list, by the way, that shrivels up in the warmth emitted by meaning.

If anything is missing in all health seminars and support groups, it's a thorough examination of the meaning of symptoms, treatment, and health. Examining the meaning of suffering brings not only peace of mind but plans of action. Ultimately, there's only one "*Health Talk*" and it includes all the rest. It's the forum on the Meaning of Health.

Genuine healing is really our last resort and our most difficult task. After we've tried everything, spent everything, or lost everything and after we are sick and tired of being sick and tired, discovering the meaning of health eases suffering on a profound level. And for those fortunate enough to have everything, whine about everything, or doubt everything but still feel as though something's missing—it's the same thing.

Still, all this talk is just driveling detail. The doors of perception open outwardly and crack open only so far when kicked in by others. The business of health is nobody's business but our own.

Can't Buy Me Love

> *We are generally more convinced by the reasons we discover on our own than by those given to us by others.*
> — Marcel Proust

By the way, while we're on the subject, the meaning of health doesn't make any business sense either. What business would survive without promising anything or doing anything? How about suggesting that we do all the work and that we'll never quite finish? But hey, that's life and that's health. The real business of health will never rate a multinational conglomerate because there is nothing to buy and nothing to sell.

Business is about finding a need and filling it, bottom line. Health care is big business because like all other multibillion dollar industries, it seeks to ease pain or provide pleasure. Fair enough. But note that gambling, alcohol, drugs, pornography, and computers are the others. There is such a thing as helping too much. When we strictly refuse all pain and seek endless pleasure, we snuff out enough stress to numb our life completely.

As a living experience, health is an exuberant and self-sufficient state of being. The healthier we are, the less we're likely to need and the less we're likely to spend. The oldest professions can survive without us. As our greed and gluttony settle, our comparing and competing cease. Then our collecting and consuming ebb naturally, as we realize that ultimately, all we need is love. Well, that all depends on what we mean by love.

The Picture of Health

This is not the kind of knowledge that you acquire,
but the kind you must become.
— Indian sage

When it comes down to it, for the most part, we're already reasonably whole human beings. So any healing, or becoming whole, begins with a mental makeover in trade for future considerations. Profound healing is something about remembering, experiencing, and identifying with what is already there.

Just how well we stand up to life's incredible woes and credible wars hints at the steepness of our road ahead. The meaning of health often sounds like a regurgitation of the "same ol', same ol'" from thousands of years of kitchen table wisdom. That's because it is. As the creator of Charlie Brown, Charles Schultz knew that "*A cartoonist is someone who has to draw the same thing everyday, without repeating himself.*"

Health is the ever growing state of relative stability in the midst of utter instability. It's a taste of inner certainty in the midst of absolute uncertainty. The meaning of health is the one thing in life that never changes—other than change.

The non-changing wisdom within ourselves is the one thing that we can count on to hang our hat and finally rest our head. Given our family, country, and the world, the meaning of health is no less than what our whole life means to us.

The meaning of health is a not passing fad, fancy, or philosophy. But it will help us make the most of the next great *cure du jour*. We don't need to wait for the last word of the Human Genome Project or Artificial Intelligence to develop our own Personal Healing Process and encourage our own Spiritual Wisdom.

Realistically, health remains an ideal that is forever our unfinished business. The idealism is to think we can wrap it up, know someone, or hire somebody to buy our way out. But to be perfectly honest, just knowing what health really means helps everything make a little more sense.

* * *

Instincts about Science and Spirit

I never did like arguing. People kept telling me that it's normal to argue. And they do it with such confidence and conviction. Yet, rarely did I see someone ever convince anybody of anything. I simply found arguing needlessly upsetting. I finally realized that it was useless arguing that really bothered me. It's not normal to be useless.

Agree to disagree? Who thinks of these things? It's OK if you're never going to see the person again. Otherwise, welcome to the same argument and growing resentment for forty years. Apologies never made any sense to me either unless you really meant it. If you're agreeing to disagree, you don't really mean it. You really think you are right and you don't care why you were arguing.

Frankly, I was probably jealous. I never knew enough to argue my point or have much of one. I wasn't confident or confrontational enough to take a stand. I would usually agree with everyone anyway, to one degree or another. Every view seemed to have some bit of truth to my way to thinking. But boy, if I ever added a little context or color to what others were saying, they would take it only as a critique and I would never hear the end of it. Without any strong opinions, I was surprised and envious that other people took their personal opinions so, uh, personally. But just to see how sacred their view or how scared the person, I took some pleasure in pushing their buttons.

With the small but diverse group of friends that I had growing up, I always found myself in the middle. Of course, each of them thought I was the extreme because compared to them I was. But I also tended to act in accordance with the company I kept—not in a manipulative way; I just found myself somewhere between the need for acceptance and the simple expression of the part of me that they understood. If I couldn't take sides and wouldn't take a stand then being the mediator felt just fine. Although the devil's advocate wouldn't be too far behind—you know, just to stimulate the discussion.

I had no internal conflict in attending scientific meetings on the one hand

and conferences on spirituality on the other. I just didn't tell anyone. All the various ideas made some sense to me in different ways. It seemed to me that both spiritual wisdom and scientific information suffered the same fate in the eyes of particularly strong viewpoints. Even the most profound wisdom is taken out of context. Still, I was always enamored by the extremes of thought, sensing that each had something meaningful to say about the middle ground, along the middle road, where I felt that I lived.

For me, some of the most inspiring writers were the older retired experts now freed from the politics, pressures, and sanctions of their institutions. Only after a lifetime of experience does the elegance of a certain modesty and modest certainty seem to emerge. Envious and impatient for this kind of wisdom, I figured I should retire as soon as possible.

The health and wellness expos produced more stress for me than offer solutions. Who could afford to listen to, buy into, or purchase all these trinkets and gadgets that absolutely guarantee a long and healthy life? I understand the bits of scientific truth and I'm interested in the ancient origins. But I have difficulty relating to just when and how these practitioners became so convinced and attached to their procedure, supplement, or philosophy. I could accept that light and sound have some subtle influences on the body but that's a far cry from the expensive magnets, ultra-sound, and infra-red gizmos deemed to cure everything.

The scientific news wasn't that much more reassuring. We're all at the mercy of the constantly changing, conflicting, and contradictory advice of medical experts. The latest treatments come and go, while miracle drugs eventually lose their magic. The pharmacist, the nurse, and the social worker all perform a different song and dance. At least the alternative healers keep their story straight. Thank God four-out-of-five dentists agree. It's hard to get good help these days.

There's no universal vernacular that speaks for the various academic disciplines. Of course, that means there are few academics that truly respect and thoroughly understand the meaning and intention of all their distant colleagues. But being an intellectual free agent, a wholesome, unbiased language is the kind of informational bang I wanted for my educational buck. I never wanted to become an expert because I'd always rather know a little something about every corner of life than everything about my little corner.

Sports medicine is a relatively recent medical discipline that tries to unite various practitioners under one roof. Physicians work alongside surgeons, psychologists, physiotherapists, and nutritionists. Still, the education, perspec-

tive, and experience of health and illness are very different in each discipline. Working in a sports medicine clinic after graduation, I could feel the subtle bias and superiority of each healer's way, even given the superficial respect and one-stop-shop convenience. Still, everyone meant well and it was good for business.

The Meaning of Science and Spirit

*To discover the truth in anything that is alien,
first dispense with the indispensable in your own vision.*
— Leonard Cohen

We can learn at least as much about the nature of flora and fauna through years of careful handling and thoughtful inspection as we can by electron microcopy or frozen section. If the absolute nature of anything is forever beyond the reach of science, then the ultimate meaning of health must be left to direct experience and keen observation. After all, we are the living truth. Where else to better inquire but within our own reflections as the living part of the reality that we are trying to understand?

There are many types of truth. There are the relatively stable and generally reliable truths found in the obvious physical and chemical laws of nature. At the other extreme, enduring truths of human subjective experience are etched in the very consistent mystical, spiritual, and historical records. Both are valid and vital, and it's fruitless to exploit one to negate the other.

The value of grasping apparently opposing truths in our head simultaneously is not generally impressed upon us. We're quite content for the most part with the categories, distinctions, and boundaries we've created for practical and functional convenience. It seems normal, necessary, and harmless to dissect science from psychology, divide mathematics from mysticism, and cultivate forestry from philosophy. But all that segregation, if taken seriously, leaves a precariously short step to mistake these abstracted maps for the actual geography.

*"As far as the laws of mathematics refer to reality,
they are not certain;
as far as they are certain, they do not refer to reality."*
— Albert Einstein

Everything is somehow related because everything originated and evolved from a single source with common elements. Matter organized everything it had into creating life, life eventually inspired minds to emerge, and then together we started building heaps more stuff. It shouldn't be too much of a debate that existence is a seamless continuum.

The continuum of all things is a varying expression of ever evolving truths, none of which are wholly independent. Individual biological, emotional, and spiritual realities are not sheltered and can't fully be understood without honoring their greater physical, cultural, and social context. The evolutionary chain from the stars in the sky to the stars in Hollywood represents the growth of concrete natural phenomena toward the ever elusive and star-struck mysteries of life and mind.

The reality of health, therefore, must encompass all the elements of nature, the common attributes of living organisms, and the universal traits of perceptive creatures. A full-bodied meaning of health then opens the discussion to include individuals, communities, and their environments.

Personality Plus

> *The real essence of the personality*
> *is the divine soul.*
> — Paul Brutan

Now as if anyone hadn't noticed, there are also different types of people. Some people are compelled to gaze in. Some people are more comfortable staring out. Different bits of the continuum ring true, come more easily, or make more sense to some people than to others. Various styles of thinking apprehend the assorted slants on reality that eventually help carve out the diverse niches of academia.

The philosophies, psychologies, and mystic traditions that are of concern to the subtle souls reside toward the softer side of reality. Physics, chemistry, and biology on the other hand, are of interest to the concrete thinkers aligning with the hard edge of existence. The complete package includes science, art, and morals—or truth, beauty, and goodness—it's all good.

If we gravitate toward the measurable laws of nature, we like predictability, black and white details, specifics, and distinctions. Mechanical cause and effect weigh heavy with us, as do analysis, experimentation, timetables, and end products. We're scientific thinkers creating a linear world for ourselves. With our feet on the ground, we see the trees.

The nice neutral facts do hold a steady structure and offer a certain practicality with which we can comprehend or ignore the vague, less straightforward evidence. At best, this orientation is rational, logical, and precise. At worst, it's arrogant and rigid, spiraling toward a stifling scientism where everything else is religiously denied. Of course, we're more likely to prevail in a competitive climate because we get things done.

Now believe it or not, there are others that actually live in a more artistic world. They are drawn to a more poetic version of life where patterns, analogies, and symbols speak the loudest. Subtle themes, relationships, and fundamental processes are obvious to them. A little artsy and a touch more earthy, they feel for the forest.

Their world provides context and depth to the bare essentials and the raw numbers. Being sensitive to the subtleties, they're more subject to the cold harshness of the cruel world. Their idealistic inclination makes it difficult in a dog-eat-dog culture and presents some problems in holding a job.

Either way or every way in between, our world appears exactly as we imagined it would. Our inner life is always recognized *out there* as familiar. Our truth readily becomes *the* truth. Our life becomes an assumption about *all* of life. The lens we use to interpret our own nature is the same lens we use to focus and filter our experience of *human* nature. In a nasty twist, the world that we create holds tremendous sway over us—especially when we forget that we just made it up.

In order to know who's who and to keep things straight, we like to classify people. We judge people by their physical features, their behavior, and their personal characteristics. Most cultures and traditions have developed some system of this personality typing. If a personality type is held to be a rigid and everlasting entity, then everything people say and do can be blamed on their personality—or excused.

Some personalities are outgoing, forward, or aggressive. Others are introspective, somewhat backwards, or passive-aggressive. Then there's everything in between. But these labels don't really tell the full story of the personality. More often than not, personality typing describes something that happened to our original disposition on the way to the psych ward.

Our adult personality is either developed, stable, and reasonably sound or it's stifled, misguided, and cranky. Inborn inclinations, talents, and tastes are invariably nurtured, cultivated, and refined or they are ignored, inflamed, and just plain mangled. Any particular methodical, emotional, or numinous personality type is fine. It's the detours and roadblocks along the personality highway that are particularly annoying, ineffectual, or dangerous. *What happened to you?*

With everyone tied to fibers of the same natural cloth, ultimately our bodies, minds, and souls are a blend of a standard fabric, differing only in the pattern, color, and concentration of truth. Some face in or out, some are roughened or smooth, but there is no such thing as an intrinsically bad personality. We may have custom woven those webs ourselves.

Can we see some ID?

Obviousness may be the ruin of the world.
— Albert Hoffman, Biologist

Just who do you think you are? Our identity determines how much of our given personality is recognized, reclaimed, and refined. During growth and development, people relate to those aspects of outer experience they deem identical with how they're feeling inside. There is a constant give and take between the truth out there and the truth in here.

As we become comfortable identifying with our preferred parts, we embrace those outstanding aspects of our personality, which then relate to similar interests out there in the world. Our identity continues to grow as we continue to grow up and it begins to gel to the extent that we stop growing. The joyous or darkened spirit we exhibit today is more a developmental function of our identity and the current manifestation of our personality than some static psychological profile. Genuine healing begins by seizing this false ID and committing ourselves to a greater potential.

Some people identify more with their outer garb. They're more apt to wrap their brain around their money, body, gender, and all their stuff. Their intellectual prowess is more enlivened and valued than any artistic bent. They may become overly extroverted, expressive, individualistic, or just plain *out there* than maybe they should've or might've.

Others differentiate themselves more by their inner nature. Values, ideas, imagination, and creativity are most important as sincere aspects of their being. Emotional about family heritage, culture, and learning, they are less attached to material things. These people might grow too reserved, receptive, flexible or just simply *far out* than they would've or could've.

Our basic personality potential existed from birth. Whatever eventually became of our personality, it was cornered and coerced by an over-identification with certain predominant features. Just how well it distinguished itself reflects our subsequent development as a person—how thoroughly we've assimilated our experiences and how rigidly we've held onto our passing persona. Original behavioral inclinations and psychological possibilities were then either funneled and restricted or guided and nurtured by family, culture, and our own perceptions to create what now looks like our personality type.

All this mutual reinforcement between us and our environment is such that our current identity eventually becomes us. Eventually, *who we think we are* is so hard-wired into our psyche that it is not easily defused. We may feel that who we can ever be is limited to who we have been so far. Resigned to this unalterable fact, we begin to make do or make excuses.

Of course, our present identity always remains a somewhat mistaken identity. It's not all bad as this perceptual apparatus is necessary to craft the diversity of disciplines. If we didn't ignore some parts of ourselves while we work or play, we'd never get anything done or have any fun—we'd be spirits or ghosts. The realization that we can alternatively utilize and enjoy different aspects of ourselves allows us to admit that we're just pretending and that there is a greater truth about who we really are.

Our true identity shines above and beyond all practical distinctions and particular interests. From this perfect perch we can oversee all sides in debates, arguments, and conflicts. We realize that any longstanding impasse usually means that different identities are engaging different types of truth from different levels of the playing field. These are category errors that can't overcome the foreign tongues of diverse ballparks. The more honestly we face the inner reaches of our own identity, the easier it is to pinpoint and reconcile these outer limits.

> *"We shall not cease from exploration*
> *And the end of all our exploring*
> *Will be to arrive where we started*
> *And know the place for the very first time."*
> — T.S. Elliot

The identity that becomes us can eventually become scary. Our views and opinions are not just views and opinions anymore. They've imploded into a cramped sense of self. Now any debates, arguments, and conflicts are taken exceedingly personal. The subtext of the confusion hardens into *us versus them* and *me versus you*. When we're fighting for our actual survival, there can be no legitimate compromise.

Most needless conflict is just conflicting personalities, but badly mangled ones. These identity issues create monumental misunderstandings, but misunderstandings nonetheless. The denied aspects of ourselves can't be recognized, related to, or relished in others. Until and unless we get over ourselves, the common ground between all people will remain buried by the surface differences. Genuine respect is forever reduced to a forced and fragile tolerance. It's difficult to believe that meaningful communication alone can resolve major confrontations until we realize that the original communication breakdown is within ourselves.

This is how we become our own worst enemy. Our disowned traits continue to hang around, secretly tormenting our obvious charm from the wings. This inner struggle is then played out one way or the other. Some types keep the strain inside, causing symptoms for themselves. If things go really poorly, they might eventually be inclined to end it all. Others redirect the pressure outwardly, causing grief and heartache for others. In the extreme, when things don't go well, their inner pressure may explode into murder.

But symptoms are symptoms and suffering within becomes everyone's sufferings. Individual struggles escalate into humanity's struggles. Much of the upset results from the psychic pushing and pulling of apparently opposing values. Our perceptions of good and bad reveal the sides of ourselves that we've chosen to accept and reject. Being *less-than-whole* is not just a metaphor. As basically forgotten selves, we often feel and act like lost and frightened souls. Our subsequent tantrums are largely responsible for the gratuitous grief around the globe.

Child development is none other than development of the identity—and the blossoming personality. The change is obvious with kids because they look and sound different every few weeks. Each year the young ones feel different inside as they navigate the constantly changing scenery. Traumatic at best, even if all goes well, inner growth begins to slow and stumble about the average level of society—the drinking age.

Now, there's no law stopping anyone from getting an identity enlargement, personality augmentation, or outlook lengthening. But generally, we're too busy with household renovations or cosmetic restorations. Parents, teachers, and city hall have done their jobs. If we feel compelled to continue our personal growth after high school or college, then we're basically on our own. We can find some support in the Human Potential Movement or the flourishing New Age encounter groups if we have the cash. For most of us, though, the limited visibility in adult life persists due to the level of fog within our perceptual world—then we become parents.

Conflicting Reports

> *In intelligent debates,*
> *both sides are right in what they affirm*
> *and wrong in what they deny.*
> — John Stuart Mill

There once were cave men; now there are lawyers. Okay, so we might understand how some people don't believe that civilization is evolving. These sticklers can't see past their own primitive self, which still exists, however sanitized. Our developing minds and evolving cultures have been playing catch up with our brainy potential ever since our knuckles left the ground.

As civilization matures, it produces more mature citizens, more or less. They become more civil to each other. The personalities haven't changed—they just grew up and became more personable. With the deeper experience of our own natural depths, we gain a more profound view of human nature in general. We can only become more humane toward each other as we notice the similarities—identifying with something in common—like our shared humanity. Then, each new and improved culture paces the development of the next generation—stops and starts notwithstanding.

The historical debate about the nature of reality is really about extreme identities arguing over the extremes of existence as one-big-thing versus one-big-thought—pure objectivity or pure subjectivity. This is the same essential dispute between mind and body, nature versus nurture, and science and religion. People identifying with *things* argue endlessly with people identifying with *thoughts*. These guys are light years apart, shooting off from different galaxies with half-loaded lasers. Without some sincere pretending, neither side can argue with a straight face.

But the fun gets out of hand when it explodes between families, communities, and countries. Gangs of certifiable experts and teams of convicted advisors fight for power, pride, or sport. It's just not very constructive.

Reconciliation requires reconciling an apparently impossible paradox. Beyond just promising and compromising more of the same, the only thing left to do is to get over themselves to honor both sides and find the meaning behind the mayhem. The misunderstanding can be resolved only with a perspective inclusive of all sides and in view of all truths.

Communication is tricky enough at the best of times with people living in the same world. Visits from other worlds take a charitable patience and a good translator. What planet did this dude come from?

An unseemly disrespect still exists between and within the religions, sciences, and the arts. You see, even the leaders take everything so personally. Listen in on the medical lounge gossip to hear what the sawbones, shrinks, and gas passers really think about each other. Defense and prosecuting mouthpieces play a similar tune on television interviews.

Diverse cultures and religions don't have a chance at peace until denominations within their own ranks patch things up. Tension between races can't relax before light and dark skinned people within the same race team up. World peace may need to wait until families can eat a meal together without upsetting some stomachs.

The exodus from western religions is not unlike the evacuation from conventional medicine. The arguing adults are disconcerting to the children. While the faithless and the impatient seem to be turning from God and science, they're not really leaving the allmighty meaning of each. They're only leaving the not-so-enlightened personalities and institutions whose biased, fragmented, and antagonistic aura has upset their innate sense of fair play.

So let the Common Health Games begin. Bring on the science and religion and the nature and nurture. Next, haul out the facts and the values, the genes and cultures, with innies and outies. As different worlds turn, different truths abound. Getting a grip on this elephant will tap all our resources of experience and experiment, analysis and analogy, surface and depths, forests and trees.

> *"...many arguments are not really a matter of better objective evidence, but the subjective level of those arguing."*
> — Ken Wilber

Meeting of Minds

> *A fully realized human being is one who knows the masculine, yet keeps to the feminine.*
> — Lao Tzu

Seeing all things in context requires an artistic application of the scientific evidence and a scientific assessment of the subjective experience. Our capacity to use everything more and waste everything less requires the utilization of all our abilities. How much we value any particular information depends on how much we value that capacity to engage in it. In a constructive dialogue, we're forced to trade any real certainty for a certain reality.

Bold and integrative movements within all disciplines are leading the way. Integrative medicine, psychology, politics, and religion are not new philosophies but bring together that which is already known. They recall the original purpose and refine the modern context. By respecting the diversity of disciplines, people, and truths as expressions of one continuum, they lead by astutely applying a wholesome truth to a whole person, culture, and environment.

Patience and modesty are required for leaders to be *trans*-cultural rather than merely counter cultural. Then they can see beyond borders, customs, and queues. A novel approach is more than a critique. It's a renovation of a cliché, dusting it off, and returning it to its original, shining glory.

Each discipline is only as applicable to people as its interpretation is integrative. Each truth is as effective and enduring as it fosters a degree of self-knowledge. This requires a learning context of love and inclusiveness, rather than one of fear and divisiveness. As the disciple's identity deepens, their perspective heightens, and worlds of meaning open up to further reveal profound and lasting truths.

Taoists say that *"Power is at the beginning."* We know that the strongest force in nature is released from the smallest nuclear bonds of atomic matter. The basic biological impulse is triggered by the genetic blueprint within the nucleus of cells. But the most subtle strength of all is the spark of creativity within the human mind which discovered, and now manipulates, both babies and bombs. It's this same sweeping power that fuels all human endeavors from scientific revelation to mystic inspiration.

> *"Nature is more like an artist than an engineer.*
> *It requires a basically artistic attitude to understand it."*
> — David Bohm, Physicist

At the edge of science toward the outer edges of space, we face a confusing mess of infinite black holes and curving space-time continuums. At the inner edge of matter, we're left with an abysmal void of zero-point emptiness, clouded with infinite probabilities and mathematical uncertainties. Not a very concrete ending to the farthest reaches of our objective inquiries.

The mysterious characteristics at the finest level of the material world sound shockingly similar to the mystical experiences describing the eternal basis of reality. The nature of mind is surely not explained by the nature of molecules. But at the same time, how can we have three separate infinities? How are the infinite vacuum of outer space and the endless void of quantum space different from the vast reaches of inner space between our ears?

In the everyday world where the math works well, we can ignore minute errors, fudge the uncertainty, and round off reality to the nearest decimal point. It all works well until it doesn't. Eventually it's hard *not* to peek into the void for ourselves. The depths of reality are really no further than the depths of our own mind and no scarier than our own life.

> *"Religion without science is blind,*
> *science without religion is lame."*
> — Albert Einstein

Followers and leaders of science and religion often lack the inventive insights and the honest intentions of the originators. Without intimate experience, all information is in danger of becoming tarnished, sanitized, dogmatic, and dumbed down to another cliché. Then, the business incentives, fashion statements, and self-serving agendas ensue to exploit the knowledge along with the innocent public. The way we use knowledge is as important as the knowledge itself.

In a desperate search for certainty and stability and in fear of disease and aging, we often cling to isolated ideas that sabotage our better judgments and best interests. But by cultivating our true identity and nurturing our full-blown personality, we are better able to understand our experience in the world to the best of our ability.

The truisms *"know thyself"* and *"heal thyself"* slyly suggest that both religion and medicine originally intended to heal the body and the soul, albeit from different directions. Religion is the social and cultural expression of what we know about subjective reality. Science is the social and cultural expression of what we know about physical reality. The meaning of health makes the most out of both to enhance our life experience. Therefore, a mature science is always compatible with a mature spirituality and the meaning of science and religion are never at odds.

Four Dimensions of Health

> *Life is not something to fix,*
> *but something to understand.*
> — Rachel Naomi Remen

All things come and go; they're born and they die; they develop and decay. The continuum of reality is a dynamic one with a constant turnover of the atoms, cells, and ideas. The staying power of each depends on a number of factors, not the least of which is the power of our attention. Cherished literature, cinema, civilizations, and sitcoms are kept alive in the hearts and minds of people. Fleeting phenomena simply do not engender enough passion—the truth, beauty, or goodness with which to identify.

The longevity of each thing requires some sustenance to sustain it. Made up of matter, life, mind, and spirit, people naturally have material, biological, emotional, intellectual, and spiritual needs. As an outgrowth of the continuum of all existence, a parallel continuum of needs emerges for personal well-being as well as cultural endurance.

Material needs are things like shelter, clothing, and safety. Biological needs are nutrients, fluids, and food energy. Emotional requirements are the love and support of others, while intellectual desires are for logic and understanding. Part of the spiritual need that makes us most human and sustains us the longest is the perception of a greater context for all the lesser needs.

The hierarchy of needs is old stuff, except that there remains a cultural bias as to the value and meaning of each level. Higher needs are seen as pampered and selfish luxuries. We forget just how much the higher necessities motivate the attainment and refine the enjoyment of the bare essentials. One needs a good reason just to get out of bed in the morning, find some work, and get some grub.

In our fixation on basic needs, we ignore and deny our highest needs, creating needless suffering. We exaggerate and overindulge our obvious needs at the expense of our subtle needs. Without a higher agenda, many symptoms, including the fixations, are unnecessarily sustained. A vicious cycle of avoidable pain spins out of a meaningless merry-go-round. When all we have is a hammer, the same pounding perspective tries in vain to soften the blows.

The emergence of mind has largely relieved us from the mechanics of biological evolution. We haven't survived this long because of our smooth skin, sweet smile, and bulging biceps. We've survived through mental cunning, if not mortal fears. Future survival, however, demands a spiritual finesse through which the environment and humanity mutually and naturally select each other. The meaning of health accepts that material and spiritual needs are mutually inclusive and equally necessary.

Often, persistent human problems are needless aggravations that reveal an imbalance of needs. The catch is that only a balanced perspective allows one to fully appreciate the needed balance. Only an identity that embraces the wide world of needs provides an equitable approach to the continuum of symptoms.

The highest human needs are under funded if only because they can't be bought. Yet the health of our careers, lifestyles, and relationships are limited only by our vision of what is truly most important—what is needed most for enduring peace and lasting pleasure.

A unified theory of health lies in the balance of the continuum of needs. Symptoms reflect a continuum of imbalances while treatment should be the balancing act. The missing link within patients and providers alike is the value given to obvious and subtle needs. We needn't achieve the perfect balance before we can recognize the importance of all our needs—we just need to see the perfection from where we are now.

Albert Einstein told us to *"Make the theory as simple as possible. But not simpler."* Four dimensions of health spontaneously appear without inventing new criteria, standards, or practices—they were always right here. Reality is naturally expressed by four living quadrants. The interior conscious experience of individuals (1) is the basis for the collective culture (2). And our physical bodies (3) are couched in the biological and material environment (4).

Looking in and looking out, all for one and one for all, the essential dynamics of Purpose, Love, Responsibility and Freedom seemingly drop into our lap. In forever increasing depths, these are the demanding experiences that fulfill the emptiness informing our imbalances, heal our identities, and seal our destinies—in more ways than one. Now, if any of the scientific gobbledygook thrown at us in high school actually stuck, we'll be demanding some objective proof about now.

Interestingly, purpose, love, responsibility, and freedom just happen to be the characteristics of longevity, happiness, and success by all academic accounts. They fulfill the epidemic emotional and spiritual void by answering the meaninglessness, powerlessness, and hopelessness that sustain chronic pain, crime, and addiction. What else could so precisely balance the highest and lowest needs of mind, body, and soul, throughout culture, society and the environment?

At the same time—miracle upon miracle—when purpose, love, responsibility, and freedom are felt at the core of who and what we are, we actually begin to embody the most inclusive interpretations of all the world's spiritual traditions. Lo and behold, these highest needs also echo the research of the latest integrative psychology, philosophy, and medicine. The experiential lens of purpose, love, responsibility, and freedom clears up a lot of esoteric wisdom and helps make sense of much of the exoteric science.

Prior to concepts, long before emotion, in another dimension of time and space, the highest needs of our essential identity are pleased by us—just being ourselves. Purpose, love, responsibility, and freedom are just the given names for the principle properties pulsating throughout all levels of reality, from rocks and stars to biological ecosystems and cultural traditions. Beyond the familiar human experience or definition, purpose, love, responsibility, and freedom are the patterns of information and energy embedded into existence.

Each of us is responsible for our own purpose and love in a way that preserves the freedom of everything else to fulfill its purpose, love, and responsibility—or nothing survives very long. An individual's world contains the purpose of his or her own conscious condition, yet always in relationship with everything else.

The Meaning of Purpose looks at why steadfast intentions serve to enliven vitality and strengthen character. The Meaning of Love demonstrates how thoughtful and careful attention has tangible healing effects. The Meaning of Responsibility begs us to pay our respects to what our lives are screaming about.

With an increasing purposeful, loving, and responsible personality we may just bump into the meaning of freedom, our ultimate identity and most challenging need. The Meaning of Freedom is as much about enjoying everything without needing anything, as it is about having nothing without lacking anything.

The meaning of health serves the spectrum of human experience and the plethora of human problems. It runs the gamut of treatments and the hierarchy of needs. The meaning of health is not always about apprehending a cure as much as comprehending the meaning of *continuity of care*. But it does give new meaning for taking that prescription "*as needed.*"

In the wink of an eye, whole new worlds open up. Understanding alone often eases suffering and enlivens healing. Meaning gives us the strength to cope with incurable conditions, helps reduce erratic choices and mistakes, and increases the chances of truly *Doing No Harm*. We're less likely to overuse, misuse, and abuse therapy when we know how to use it wisely.

And it's all as simple as that, but not as easy as all that. We'll never cure everything or finish fixing our lives but one never knows what else we'll discover. The mad dash for health diminishes as we breathe easy just knowing where to begin.

Healing is, after all, a pen versus sword thing. The war on drugs, the fight against cancer, and the battle of the bulge all make for a lot of unproductive combat and strenuous fencing. Use a pen. When faced with a crisis, realize that we've been fighting all along. It's now time to work smarter rather than harder. With the spiritual armaments of purpose and freedom we can finally put down our weapons to begin a sincerely loving response.

* * *

Insights on Purpose

I never knew exactly what I wanted to do with my life. But I knew for sure that it shouldn't feel like a chore. I wasn't even interested in being happy—I wanted to do something meaningful. It was fascinating and compelling to see the energy and confidence in people who were fascinated and compelled by their work. They must know what they're doing.

The parental refrain, "Because I said so," didn't seem like a good enough reason to do anything. Still, I had to assume somebody knew what was going on. The height advantage, forceful tone, and experience carved in their faces were convincing enough. Given the benefit of my doubt, I knew that I would eventually grow up and then I would know what I'm doing and why.

In the meantime, I did what I was told. I followed my older brother around, played the same sports, listened to the same music, and tried to pal around with his friends. From my appointed twenty yards back, I wondered how he knew what to do.

The true meaning of Christmas, like the meaning of every holiday, escapes us more often than not. The presents, the parties, and the pomp distract from the purpose. I disliked that the pageantry was usually more important than the people or the idea we're supposed to be honoring. Still, the time, angst, and attention to the details always stole the show. To me, the relationships were the thing. I guessed that the more meaningful the relationships, the less money probably spent on making such a big production.

If it's the thought that counts, shouldn't you put some into it? I spend too much time just choosing the right cards for people. People always want to go in with you, get the secretary to send something, or phone for some registered item. Without much thought, there's little pleasure or point in it—it doesn't count. Of course, there's still "good things come in small packages." I'd rather receive a token gift that really meant something to somebody.

You begin to lose hope when medical school doesn't quite do it for you. Third year is a tricky transition, the link between books and patients. My school squeezed it into four months. I got a little jet-lagged and failed the mid-term exam. When I passed the oral retest the following week, I refused to accept it, citing they didn't know what they were doing. They thought they'd found the missing link.

 I became cranky with everyone for not being as outraged at the widespread lack of purpose as I was. Now parents, professors, and patients were the targets of my self-righteous sarcasm. It was meaningless to them. My poorly made point was affecting my work. Good thing I wasn't going to work—not really. Not until I knew what I was doing and why. Maybe Dad was right about the contempt.

 I never really tried my hardest or did my best at anything. Nothing spoke to me or maybe I just couldn't hear. Writing became my saving grace, a way to express outrage and resolve grievances. I shocked myself by working my hardest...and loving it. Writing this book is the only work that ever really had my full heart. When you have a strong purpose, maybe you naturally become good at something.

The Meaning of Purpose

*One's destination is never a place,
but rather a new way of thinking.*
— Henry Miller

Children have more to say than simply the darndest things. If parents aren't too tired to care what it means, the kids' natural curiosity and incessant questioning might seem reminiscent of a passion lost. With a little patience and a lot of respect, the endless begging *why, why, why* of the little tykes begins to make sense.

Persistent pestering is not the intellectual inquiry of a young Einstein, but the spontaneous, emotional yearning for learning. Suggesting that children suppress the urge, or demanding that they deny it, is like forcing the little rug rats to sit still. But we do it.

Fortunately, this instinctive appetite to make sense of things doesn't die. It just hibernates with all gut instincts in a harsh climate that cries out that *"This is the way things have always been done."* Only the rare creative leader or youthful adventurer seems charmed, lucky, or stubborn enough to counter the cult of a commanding culture. They boldly march to their own distinct drumming, following inspired rhythms as if possessed by a childlike wonder.

The young mind is reasonable in its appeal for reason. A child's sense of self-worth is honored by honest answers to these humble requests. This self-importance fuels the child's eagerness to achieve any outside goals—now *also* important. As an adult, the trick (as it were) to feeling a sense of purpose is not to force it, read into it, or blindly accept it. If we can awaken our innate *Rip Van Wonder*, then purpose in life will be there for the taking.

Purpose is defined as the means to an end. It's the product or the goal—the end result. As such, it lives in the future. Our intent to achieve some ensuing event, or to avoid some previous episode, is a present wish for a future desire. We may not know if our lifelong dreams are worthwhile until we attain them. By then it might be too late. Add to that the idea that our dreams and dreads are merely assumptions or guesses at best—so much for definitions.

Meaning on the other hand lives in the present. Rather than a means to an end, meaning is an end in itself. The brilliant significance and glowing relevance of present endeavors are recognized *right now*. Meaning is realized in the mutual influence and panoramic light of everything else.

Since everything is connected, there's always an elusive array of short and long term effects—the subtle and obvious outcomes of actions. The interplay of physical, emotional, social, and cultural dominos allows for ample meaning for all things considered in our approach.

At some point, most people wonder about what their life's purpose might be. But until we find what is meant for us, or figure out what we'd love to do, at the very least, our plans should include staying awake and hanging around long enough to seize the day, if and when it ever comes by.

The Nature of Purpose

Science cannot solve the ultimate mystery of nature
and that is because in the last analysis
we ourselves are part of the nature,
and therefore part of the mystery that we are trying to solve.
— Max Planck

As the awakening part of nature and having lost touch with much of our instincts, we're forced to ponder our possible purpose. Since meaning is found in the greater context, our fundamental purpose includes a keen awareness of our strategic placement amongst all material, living, and thinking things.

But first, purpose insists we get to know all of our own attributes—just becoming ourselves. It means developing our capabilities to the best of our abilities by tapping all inner and outer resources. In the light of this immediate purpose, all our challenges can be made meaningful.

All endeavors also become meaningful when guided by this ever-present intent. Purpose is elevated to an ongoing process rather than just an end product. Cultivating purpose is an end in itself—it's the way we live our lives on a day-to-day basis. Released from the anxiety, anticipation, or let-down of the final results, the pure satisfaction of *just knowing why* makes everything we do instantly worthwhile. The clichéd *journey* indeed finds validation over the privileged *destination.*

The gnawing aimlessness and the not so quiet desperation that sustains many symptoms is reason enough to unearth our unexamined lives. Layers of warm-blooded meaning are more soothing than cold-blooded survival—just getting by. The satisfaction of *significance* works to refine the quality and balance the quantity of our lower survival needs. The explosive array of need and greed is defused in a blast of purpose—understanding why.

As purpose in daily life comes alive, spontaneity becomes our constant companion. Purpose is the natural act of our identity baggage just waiting to be claimed. Hormonally inclined males have historically been granted such strong intentions. But biological distinctions dissolve with the equal opportunities that higher human aims provide. By the time our spiritual hunger has us ravishing for a greater serving of human potential, wherever we go, the meaning precedes us.

When we begin to make sense of our world, new worlds suddenly appear. And they all make a little more sense. The mundane becomes miraculous, the routine becomes sacred, and everyday life becomes a worthwhile experience. It's meaningful because we're learning about ourselves in context of everyone else.

By all means, check out what the world's religious offerings have to say about purpose. It's a wonder anybody knew anything thousands of years ago. Never mind that the world's oral and written scriptures still stand up today, revealing bigger truths each time we read them—or maybe we just notice more.

The various wisdom traditions provide many conceptions of life's purpose. The most enlightened interpretations though require a perception equal to those who originally perceived the words. In the meantime, intellectual and philosophical inquiries alone aren't enough to sustain the daily feeling-tones necessary for an enduring purpose. Somewhere between literal commandments and esoteric metaphors, we're left to experience our purpose for ourselves.

The state of global affairs doesn't inspire much confidence. The original countries of the world's greatest scriptures seem the least likely to live up to them. The increasingly secular western world mutually antagonizes a resistive fundamentalist third world, with deadly consequences. It's ironic that fighting over the world's holiest sites may just wipe them out, and with that, the long lost reasons behind the hostilities. Both extremists await a meaningful vision to lead them out of temptation—to fight.

Living itself often provides the wherewithal to grasp the intent of the spiritual texts. Over time, growing individual awareness and the natural evolution of culture leads to a more civilized world. Citizens, as they become worldly, recognize the common value and modern relevance in the written words of all cultures for all peoples. It must say that in there somewhere?

Curiously, many religions interpret our fate as forever cast out of nature. It does often appear that way and we tend to get a little insecure. The poor, thinking part of nature is mostly the scared part. Granted, we bear the burden of figuring out what to do next, while the rest of the species seem to know instinctively. Individually, our mistaken identity may well be our original sin. Then our original blessing and final redemption would be one and the same—the wholly directed purpose toward our true identity.

The Purpose of Nature

Energy = Matter
— Albert Einstein

Without projecting our ethnocentric wishes and New Age dreams upon humble matter, we can admit that quantum physics offers some legitimate insight into nature's design. Subatomic stuff is found to be simultaneously schizoid and wise. Resonating like waves of light, the essence of matter leaves particulate traces, when in fact it is neither.

At its finest, solid material exists as peculiar patterns of ordered information. Depending on what country, culture, or decade we peek through, that information exerts itself as a variety of ethereal particles and energy force fields.

This information has characteristics that are more substantial than the boring impression of matter. It reveals self-organizing and self-sustaining tendencies, as if it knows something, has something to do, and somewhere to go. This self-fulfilling, self-directed quality accounts for the increasing order in natural phenomena.

The molecular level of things is no less interesting—for keeners. Objects hold their magnificent structure and precise function in spite of continuous turnover of component parts. Nebulous quantum particles blink in and out of existence, while the pattern permits the atomic intent to be energetically maintained, like a frozen chunk of light. Physical things fulfill their functional purpose to remain solid entities so that we can sit down without falling down.

Chaos and Systems Theories try to paint a coherent picture of nature by the numbers, we might say. The sciences of Simplicity and Complexity search for the math behind madness (not required reading). While the decimals are inevitably fudged by constants and us constantly rounding off numbers, some rudimentary designs are suggested.

At the biological level, the beauty, precision, and marvel of every shape, color, and size take center stage. The wildly colorful camouflaging chameleon, the spider web's steel-like strength, and the incredible transparency of the eyeball's cornea are all child's play in nature's engineering handbook. These *teleological* designs fulfill their function better than any human plans, as if they were meant to be. Romantic notions aren't necessary to appreciate this functional purpose—no matter how randomly mutated the selections.

The instinct of all bacteria, plant, or animal to live and prosper underscores a universal dynamic that lives and breathes throughout existence. Termed *auto-poesis*, this self-determined tendency is a fundamental feature that informs all cells and living systems how to fulfill their destiny. Tending to be, if not intending to be, all things do their thing.

Life, taken in isolation, appears quite content going nowhere. Without any intention of further evolution, the fittest creatures are the microbial wonders that weigh in as the majority of the bio-mass. Bacteria are continuously found in the most inhospitable places on earth, without oxygen or sunlight, and have survived the various mass extinctions. Yet life remains couched in the universal development of basic elements getting more complex and organized, becoming more alive and more thoughtful—as if it had something in mind.

Human purpose after all, requires a mind. Any intent that animals may have, whatever insight plants might harbor, or interiority atoms possess requires some big-time mind reading. The age-old desire for a *designing intelligence* behind the façade of reality must await a personally divined intervention. Meanwhile, the fractal geometry of molecules, mountains, and mole hills remains really, really neat.

The evolution of our own perception determines how evolutionary the outer world appears. Our developmental awareness determines the level of awareness that we in turn ascribe to plants and pets. The more purpose that we experience indoors, the more purpose we'll recognize outdoors.

Science, by definition and time constraints, is compelled to ignore the meaning of things in order concentrate on the mechanism of things. Both scientific and religious exercise can whither into dried instruction and feeble execution, only to be further dehydrated by our interpretations.

Remember that like us, both science and religion get bogged down with day-to-day affairs, rituals, ceremonies, circumstances, and funding. In the hands of ordinary people, the purpose often gets mistaken by someone who cares less. Experts are as likely as us to forget the basic intent that inspired the coveted theories, insights, and revelations. The highest value of ancient and modern realizations is most certainly there, but it patiently awaits our budding wisdom.

Advancing physics peers into the subtlest mechanisms at the farthest reaches of matter and space. If we're human, we can't help but contemplate the precision, the perfection, and the purpose. The physics of consciousness peeks into the personal space that holds meaning for the farthest reaches of personal matters. The meaning of purpose lives before all the concepts we create, prior to the precepts we preach, to be actualized in our subjective awareness.

The biggest lessons from science and religion are the ones hardest to teach—the value of our own spiritual inspiration and scientific revelation. This ultimate purpose, not given its due, easily undermines any perfunctory purpose. The meaning we experience *in here* is all we have to get our heads around any meaning we exhume *out there*.

Fulfilling our purpose is not another rule to follow, but rather rules that follow us. These are not new principles to memorize, but principles to remember are already in place. Purpose happens when we stop searching where the light is and peer into the darkened laboratory of our own inspired shadow.

Purpose at the Level of the Body

> *If you keep busy enough,*
> *you don't have to face your life.*
> — Rodney Dangerfield

Use it or lose it. Stop to smell the roses. The clichés will end when we remember what they mean. Fulfilling physical needs is as vital to well-being as the higher needs. While it's acceptable to honor nutritional needs, security concerns, and the bare essentials, any serious sensual and recreational needs are considered a luxurious, spa-like indulgence. When we're busy being busy with more important things, it's common to be out of touch with the body's desires. If the suggestion of fully engaging the body as part of our purpose seems like nonsense, maybe we've lost our senses.

Like the perfect pecs, the subtle sense of smell, taste, and sound shrivel up with the libido if they're not exercised regularly. Inactivity and under-stimulation has diminished our sensual awareness more than the evolutionary shrinkage alone.

Sharpness of hunger and satiety cues, alertness to the signs of fatigue, and early signals of pain and disease are the benefits of a finely tuned biological specimen. Bodily purpose begins with a thorough appreciation of its range of sensitivity for pain and pleasure. Just to revel in the pure physicality of a well balanced form is one of life's simple pleasures. Physically fulfilled and biologically polished, the body will be the spitting image of a well-oiled, lean, mean machine.

The body requires routine rotation of all its parts and services to remain effective, efficient, and alive. This means scratching and sniffing as many things as possible. Purpose here is about looking and really seeing, touching and actually feeling, listening and truly hearing, and eating and finally tasting. Sensory deprivation wouldn't be used as torture if it wasn't known to break our will.

With a newfound respect, patience, and deliberateness for the full range of ambient temperatures, aroma, and flavors of natural surroundings, a sensual life takes on vital importance. This attention to home and office naturally finds the colors, smells, sounds, and textures that pacify stress, settle fidgeting, and calm nerves.

It's not therapy yet, but an inspired way to live every day. Full sensory living acts to soothe the senses, calm the cravings, and ease the irritations while breathing life into the shrunken appendages. Why torture ourselves? And of course, the more we attend to the senses on a daily basis, the less we'll spend on spa attendants.

Muscles, being what they are, need to move. The more we move them, the more they'll motivate us. The more varied activities and postures we assume, the more we'll recognize our best playing weight without any high-tech measures or magazine quizzes. All types of physical recreation and disciplines remind us of muscles we didn't know we had and strength we didn't realize possessed us. All this shuffling is just normal care and maintenance—our purpose at the level of the body.

With growing body awareness, our strengths and weaknesses, gifts and gaffs, eccentricities and idiosyncrasies may nudge some buried sense of biological purpose. When we honor the body's precision, take pride in its beauty, and identify with its style, then all earthly pleasures become a little more beautiful. A harmful hedonism holds to mindless fun with reckless abandon and aggressive avoidance. On the other hand, a healthy hedonism offers meaningful fun and festivities of lasting value in the widest context, with the best of intentions. When we're comfy in our own skin, even our ulterior motives become altruistic.

The body has some free reign and will take care of business while we're out. But if we want the brain to be onside for our higher pursuits, then we'll have to respect the biology. Our indulgent fixations begin to exhaust some cortical senses while we tend to ignore the rest. Cultural taboos and personal fears inhibit behavior and choices to further stifle the sense organs. Eventually, the body protests with the sensitivities, irritabilities, allergies, and atrophies that reinforce our limited focus.

Without ever knowing the glory of physical and sensual fitness, we might find all this meaningless. Like blaming our personality, we've resigned ourselves to a body that looks like some pre-owned wreck. Our felt-experience has conditioned us that a reconditioned model is out of the question. Identifying with our slovenly, slouchy, and sloppy selves, we're convinced that it's definitely in the genes. Until we're certain of a higher physical purpose, our true animal potency remains to be seen. Then when we know what we're dealing with, we won't simply accept what we've been dealt.

Sensual knowing opens the doors of perception to the wealth of physical well-being. This doesn't mean we must be a professional athlete or be obsessed with our mirror image. We may indeed lean towards an intellectual or contemplative bent. Still, the physical familiarity can't help but inspire some ideas, relieve a few sticking points, and provide the stepping stones for whatever drives our crank.

The day-to-day indulgence of corporeal needs is an end in itself—part of our lifetime membership package. Beyond looking good and feeling great, the immediate meaning of sensual needs is realized only in context of a still higher purpose. If this all sounds a tad self-absorbed, recall that we need to truly *know, experience, and identify* with our body so it won't drag us down—so we can finally get over it and get on with it.

Remember too, that the brain is part of the body and therefore included in the calming and settling of the physiology. We may just become clear and concerned enough to think of something really great to do with our lives. Realize as well, that sensual awareness is actually a subjective discipline. Psychological healing then continues naturally along with our purpose beyond our exclusive identity with the body.

Purpose at the Level of the Mind

> *Sincere motivation is the greatest antidote*
> *for fear and anxiety.*
> — Dali Lama

Reading, 'Riting, and 'Rithmetic of course are the compulsory R's for surviving in a concrete jungle. Rationality and reason are more valued and pay better than imagination and intuition. *"Put on your thinking caps, put down your crayons, and stop daydreaming."* This cultural bias against the full spectrum of thought twists the last tie on any irrational rubbish that we haven't yet cleared from our minds.

But psychological refinement demands that we confront this restrictive conditioning of education and culture. Non-rational thinking is not the same as irrational thinking. All business and scientific thought is supported by creativity, passion, and gut feelings. If we are bored and unimaginative, then our logic suffers. Similarly, without reason, our dreams and fantasies remain flighty.

The range of subtle insights, artistry, and emotional expression is as imperative as logic, deduction, and the more concrete, formal operations. All are equally needed for mental fulfillment and to temper any obsessions, aversions, and distractions. A well-balanced cerebral life perks up the success and enjoyment of anything else to which we put our minds.

The more we relate to the various ways of the mind, the diversity of disciplines will increasingly speak to us. We're only as cultured as our ability to consider other ideas, people, and cultures. With the patience to reflect on all the notions that attract and repel, excite and bore, we may just recognize something important about ourselves. We may even shake loose some hidden passion.

The more we directly *know, experience, and identify* with the extreme workings of our own mind, the more we can relate to the extremes of art and science and appreciate the roots of far out philosophies and radical religions. The common mental blocks to living, learning, and loving can be patiently expected, respected, and resolved. Often, the simple treatment for our ailing mind is to re-engage heartily in our purpose at the level of the mind.

Learning is an end in itself. Knowing a little nothing about everything rounds out our personality more than knowing everything about almost nothing. We might just drop the attitude that hinders true wisdom and soften the sharp-tongued vitriol that disrespects others.

Before we go completely out of our minds, remember that these mental gymnastics act to invigorate and revitalize any stinkin' thinkin' or rot thought. It's not therapy—yet. It's the normal routine for an integral healer. Knowing the plain and simple truth of all our subjective skills is the only logical way to experience the meaning of mental well-being.

Before becoming preoccupied with being so self-occupied, remember our still higher purpose. Balancing the mind eases the emotions and satisfies the intellect as it relieves the *pull me, push you* of psychic tension. We may even forget the obsessions and befriend the aversions that have grabbed our attention and captured our imagination. Beyond the exclusive identity with thoughts about ourselves, we may just be inspired to some divine purpose.

Purpose at the Level of the Soul

The most beautiful thing we can experience is the mysterious.
It is the source of all true art and science.
— Albert Einstein

Finding oneself is a New Age cliché, but losing oneself in work is a time-honored tradition. If we're buried in fitness, recreation, or work we might be hiding from something upsetting—like our meaningless life. To know the feeling of completely being ourselves is both the means and the ends of our ultimate purpose.

Now, if we knew exactly what the soul was, we might just have something here. At least there's that part of us that never changes or ages. That familiar witness of our running narratives and color commentaries is the same at seven and at seventy, offering the hint of a saving grace. Whatever becomes of our God-forsaken personality and our decadent physique, it's still us.

The quintessential *"I"* is a lot more than the persona and the package. We have ideas and sensations without actually being those perceptions. As the observer of objects and subjects, we are in essence the mysterious entity holding onto all our foolish ideas, lugging around that bag of bones.

Somewhere beyond pure objectivity and pure subjectivity is the pure being that experiences both. As the thinker of thoughts and sensor of sensations, we already have an idea of our natural identity. Here, where perception is the highest, meaning is the deepest.

In a moment of total absorption, any activity becomes a soulful experience. Dancing, singing, writing, and romancing are most invigorating when we lose track of time and place. But there's a fine line between losing oneself in an object of desire and just trying to get away from it all—they kind of look the same. It all depends on our intentions.

Our soulful purpose is to *know, to experience, and to identify* with the inner space where art is first seen, songs are first heard, and facts are directly revealed. It's in this fountain of inspiration where we become an expert songwriter, philosopher, or painter—no matter what others think.

A spiritual purpose, however romanticized by cinema or ignored by schools, offers the most wholesome side effects. Special talents and unique gifts emerge from the originality and the genius of this most resourceful resource. The sense that this vocation or that avocation is meant for us seems too good to be true. We feel hardly deserving as it just fell in our lap, yet we can't imagine doing anything more authentic. *Good work if you can get it.*

Other people can give us a lot of pleasure and reason for living, but no one can give us the intimate high of being on purpose. There's nothing more life-giving than the genuine creative process, where whole images, stories, and revelations explode in a spiritual climax. Purpose at the highest level makes all life experience feel worthwhile and gives us an undying source of unassuming confidence.

This subtle empowerment provides the intellectual conviction and the emotional fearlessness to smile in the face of sacrifice, laughter, or critique. Those charmed enough to express that which most others have suppressed are likely to endure some teasing, ridicule, or scorn along the way.

The absolute faith in our deepest purpose importantly earns us the respect that we can now give to the spontaneous expertise of innate healing mechanisms. The finest taste of purpose's self-fulfilling dynamic gives us the calming certainty and whole-hearted trust that everything will eventually work out for the best.

We're just fulfilling our evolutionary purpose by being someone real, knowing something true, and going somewhere sure. The seeds of kinship with the self-sustaining purpose of everything else are securely planted.

Even our personality prospers in the midst of this newly minted identity. By identifying with *why* we do everything that we do, we embody the ubiquitous principle of purpose. Reborn now, as the personification of truth, the incarnation of meaning, and spirit of health, our will to live was never so strong.

The Will to Live

> *A man with a why to live for,*
> *can survive almost any how.*
> — Viktor Frankl

Everyone has some idea about the will to live. That's why we named it. The will to live is most apparent in the anecdotes from POW survivors and those overcoming the incredible odds of massive injuries or severe illness. Inevitably, the will to live reveals the inspiring pursuit of a passion, the honoring of a personal commitment, or the reconnection with a loved one. This driving incentive supposedly fuels the wherewithal to thrive in the face of life threatening conditions, overwhelming losses, and the worst inhumanity.

Exactly how this emotive force translates into biological stamina is not scientifically certain. It eludes rational scrutiny because there is no precise biological mechanism. We can't measure the will to live, guarantee it, or even be sure of our own until it's provoked. And for every stirring story there are a million sad ones. Without a *will pill* to buy, sell, or prescribe, the will to live remains an intriguing oddity at the very edge of health science.

But we don't need a new biological mechanism. The normal and natural stress-relaxation response is itself a physiological expression of our identity in purpose. Each step in our identity steps up the personality of our physiology, as it were. This new baseline metabolism represents a refinement of tension within the psyche. Each particular body type is inclined to a certain metabolic profile, which is then modified or mollified as it merges with succeeding new levels of awareness in purpose.

The will to live is the perceptual mind-set of the person who seriously embodies a deep sense of purpose. Subsequently and subconsciously, their full intentional essence is then powerfully articulated by their physiology. In spite of immediate or lasting stress, this *intentionality* literally refreshes the biological will with an equivalent *cellular* fortitude.

We notice the will to live only in times of crisis, and in retrospect, because the person actually lives to talk about it. But if the will to live retrieves us from the brink of death, it must be doing something when we're out shopping till we drop. Our will to live either exists or it doesn't. Popping in like Superman to save the day stretches even the most pliable imagination. If the will to live can add years to our life, it must be adding life to our years.

This *willingness* to live is evidenced daily by the liveliness in our step, the gleam in our eye, and the song in our heart. It acts as a constant physical conditioning force that exists before, during, and after our death-defying turmoil. This force of will, though, is anything but forced. The perceptual advantage we've gained by a purposeful life translates into a spontaneous and natural way in the world.

Obesity, smoking, and a sedentary lifestyle can't account for the everyday experience and conflicting evidence that we witness with our friends and neighbors. Everyone's heard of a heavy smoker who has outlasted a vegetarian marathoner. The well-accepted risk factors for longevity fade in importance during the century that centenarians live out their moderate but diverse lifestyles. The confounding cofactor is an immensely profound purpose, which isn't recorded, controlled, or ruled out in the studies. So our reason for being, our *raison d'etre*, is not that unreasonable.

But willful purpose is something of a double-edged sword. If society values what we do, we're a hero until the skills or charms deteriorate. We should take the self-respect and self-worth while we can get them. But, if we identify exclusively with what we do, then the respect and worthiness retire when we do, change when the trends change, and drop when the stock market falls. A crisis of fame and fortune means yet another identity crisis.

We envy the athletes, entrepreneurs, and entertainers for their gift, the love of what they do, and their exciting lives. But when they believe their own hype, when they can't walk away, and their skills fade with the applause, they can turn into their own caricature. The will to live often dies with the dream.

This *act of will* can kill as surely as it can heal. It won't do us in immediately without some drastic attempts because the body has a willingness of its own. But over time, a conflicted will strangles the cellular will of the body, just as the scattered will of humanity tends to antagonize the will of the planet.

Just as we're always already whole, we never really lose our *joi de vivre*. It's in there somewhere. In dire straits, the possibility exists that we could pull the brute strength of will out of a hat. But odds are better if we're prepared.

The maturing personality is more apt to identify with the meaning of things, rather than with the things in themselves. Any past glories survive but not as longings and yearnings for the good old days. Past successes live and breathe as legendary expressions of what the person's life means right now. The meaning in our lives never tires or retires, so the *will to meaning* endures no matter what fate befalls our careers.

Integrity and Character

> *Integrity simply means the willingness not to violate one's identity.*
> — Eric Fromm

Integrity is simply the essential nature of a whole person. Just as integers are whole numbers and integral psychology is holistic in scope, the integrated life embraces body, mind, and soul—*together again for the first time*. We'll know because our emotions, intellect, dreams, and behavior are all facing the same direction, toward the same ends, with the same means, for the benefit of the whole.

Everything we do, think, feel, and desire effortlessly align. Without second guessing or any cross purposes, we smoothly come to swift decisions. Conscious intent is not undermined by subconscious fears. We still make mistakes, but we come by them honestly—apology accepted.

The subsequent strength of our character is the same inner strength that emboldens our performance. This is the power that provides the privilege to stand up for what we deem most important. Resisting temptations is not necessarily a strenuous effort because we're simply not very interested. We innocently embody the characteristics of an integrated identity and a balanced personality.

Character is not a force of will either, but rather a force of habit. It's a *spontaneous will*. We legitimately intend to heed our ultimate best interests rather than any immediate selfish needs. We're following an internal guidance system that is respectful of the authority and sacred commands but with a conscience that makes the behavior authentic. It's not even particularly heroic to be virtuous because it's so personally satisfying. This is not the exclusive nature of a particular personality type but natural way of a whole and stable one.

It's considered criminal to hurt others and a sickness to hurt oneself. But both behaviors are similarly *out of character*. The discrepancy within such an assassinated character tilts *any* type toward their more insidious inclinations and tenacious tendencies. It's the tight confines of the stunted persona that tend to exaggerate normal expressions and inflame natural instincts.

We can't legitimately teach, legislate, or enforce integrity and character. These developmental traits develop naturally, like walking and talking, in an environment where people honestly walk and talk. They have no purpose to lie.

Values and Ethics

> *A man is only as good as what he loves.*
> — Saul Bellows

Parents scold children as they punish them: "*You know better than that.*" Well, everyone *knows* better on an intellectual level—even the parents. But we don't *do* better because we don't *feel* like it. When our heart adopts knowledge directly, moral ideas turn over into valuable emotional currency that insures our ensuing behavior, now a natural commodity.

Only a disintegrated purpose could sustain the selfish motives that recklessly drive one's detoured behavior. No amount of lecturing, bribing, and punishing will heal the apathy, fatigue, and fear that accompany pointlessness.

True values and ethics are widely displayed in all daily choices. Try as we might, our actual lived values are usually a tad off our professed, prescribed, or promised values. In the heat of the moment, our true colors betray our imagined values. Our values and ethics, then, simply reveal the spontaneous behavior that is on par with a particular personality type at a particular level of development in a particular culture—a sign of the times and one's timely character.

Like our current physiological profile, our actions are manifestations of deep-seated feelings about what is good and what is bad—for our immediate purpose. For all intents and purposes, our moral judgment parallels our judgment in helping or hindering our personal needs. What we perceive as valuable for our present-day purpose always undercuts any recollections of what is commonly known to be best for physical, mental, and spiritual well-being. For better or worse, this is the same benchmark we use to judge the best interests of those we care about.

Society portrays a picturesque image of moral values, but our collective conduct gives us away. Institutionalized gambling, runaway fast foods, communal cyber-sex, and cosmetic cures run amok because these are the things we indeed value most—the lowest means to the highest ends ($). This may not present any immediate danger, but it's a clear and present message of what we prefer. Young citizens are then molded subliminally by these suggested retail values much more than by any public service announcements to the contrary, higher values.

When we're engaged in public debate or dialogue, any true convictions that we utter stem from this inner monologue of values. Anything else, and most of what is said, is rote, rehearsed, and ridiculous. This is never more evident than when the disgraced spiritual, social, and civic leaders walk through the hallowed halls of shame hanging their heads.

As purpose is pursued, character and integrity naturally ensue—and so ensues our relationship with everything else. There is no way around it. As we fulfill our purpose, even our subconscious behavior reflects the higher values. If purpose, as stated here, seems too rugged and individualistic, then we've forgotten the continuum of all things. Since nothing exists in isolation, our personal purpose lovingly blends into the same organic brew with familial, cultural, and global purpose.

* * *

Imagining Love

There's something about extraordinarily nice people that was always intriguing and attractive to me. Their comforting voice, easy manner, and welcoming eye contact were exceptional. Their unexpected acceptance was a shocking reminder of how unaccepting I must be. They seemed happier than most people. They must know something. I'd be nicer too if I had a clue what I was doing. Wouldn't everyone want to become like this if they knew how?

I always thought of women as smarter, nicer, and cleaner than me—the whole sugar and spice thing. Before much cultural conditioning, at age four I was in love with my neighbor who remains my image of beauty and class. Some things never change. She smiled with her whole face. Her large white teeth and dark brown eyes on mocha skin were no less appealing with her habit of eating crayons.

It's true that I didn't grow up with the Cleaver's, the Brady's, or in Little House on the Prairie. But Ralph and Alice, Fred and Wilma, and Hi and Lois were not that far off. Dad buried himself in the paper while Mom scampered and fussed about. When I'm married, I promised Mom, I will crank up the stereo and we'll zoom through the housework together. She laughed as she shoved my feet with the vacuum and I craned around her toward the television.

Growing up at a time when only one kid at school had divorced parents, I had a pretty good opinion of love and marriage. I considered myself a hopeful romantic. The stories of happy endings for high school sweet-hearts really appealed to me. I didn't have commitment issues as much as I felt that I had little to promise. Still, I definitely didn't have the cool to pull off the playboy role. So either way, I was screwed—or not.

But I thought a lot about love. I assumed that when one idiot says *I love you*, the other idiot echoes the sentiment. I assumed it has to be mutual or it's not love. Unrequited love must be loneliness, lust, or dreaming about lust. How well can you know someone and what is the appeal if they won't have any-

thing to do with you? Being invisible was always enough for me to get the message and get out.

Granted, I went too far to the other extreme. I would approach a girl only if not-too-subtle hints were banging me over the head—like her approaching me. That was my type. I mean, why bother people? My limited self-image limited the girls that I could imagine would be interested. Playing hard to get seemed like a surprisingly odd routine. Girls are already hard to get. With this kind of un-cool, I'm sure I had a couple of soul mates walk in and out of my life.

Asking for a commitment seemed pointless to me. I mean, if you have to ask.... I had good reason not to commit. Why would I? I had no idea what I was doing and I wasn't all that nice about it. It was always a shock and a miracle when the occasional soul saw something in me that I knew didn't exist.

Cheating on girlfriends was never a problem, but for purely selfish reasons. Who needs the grief? Not to mention the burden, the guilt, the secrecy—please, just break up already. With my low self-esteem, when finally persuaded that someone actually wanted to be with me, I couldn't hurt them like that. But I always assumed that I'd meet the person I was supposed to meet when I became the person I was supposed to become.

I presumed that true love never dies. Love is mutual and love is forever. Well, it sounds good on paper. True, the real deal is an ideal, but if fades away, then it was probably something else. Maybe fun, worthwhile, and good practice, but that's not the big "L." You know for sure just how real it is only when you finally die trying—the whole death-do-you-part thing. Talk about going together.

Watching celebrities walk away from the world's beautiful people made me think that any list I had of things I like in a woman is likely useless. I reckoned that when you had to be together no matter the annoyances, grievances, and inconveniences, then it might be love.

There's no question that my generation has done a hatchet job on marriage. Not that the old institution didn't require some major repairs. But still, how pathetic. Yet people who stay together are not necessarily happier than divorced people, and more often than not, more than a little bit jealous. Sometimes it might be more loving to leave, or less loving to stay. As a former child myself, I find that people are too cavalier about the collateral damage they inflict on children when they break up. Kids today will probably reverse the trend of their childish parents, who reversed the trend of theirs.

I've thought about being gay. Not for me, of course. I mean, I was intrigued by the phenomenon once I got over being disturbed by it. Something about gender identity had something to teach me about gender and identity. Male and female, masculine and feminine didn't tell the whole story about boys and girls. I realized I loved female singers with deep masculine voices and male singers with high falsettos. I preferred women professionals and male artists. I knew many macho female athletes who could beat the crap out of as many effeminate guys. And I'd always rather get into the girls' conversation in the kitchen than watch the game with the boys—ulterior motives notwithstanding.

My desire for kids was tempered by my insistence that I be a decent role model. This may take some time. It seemed cruel and unusual to see kids being dragged through stores, the perfect height for toys and candy, then being expected to behave as adults. Parents didn't think twice about cursing drivers, neighbors, and each other in front of their kids. I was furious with parents who smoked and argued while infants hung off one arm. People who admitted the challenge and humbly resisted having kids seemed to consider the children's needs more seriously than their own. I wondered if they would make the best parents.

The Meaning of Love

*The plain and simple truth about love
is rarely plain and never simple.*
— George Bernard Shaw

Love is a many splendored thing—so they say. Well, it's a lot more than words can say. The poets, singers, and songwriters give it their best shot, but not before stuffing a few divorces, custody battles, and restraining orders under their belts. Often reduced to hopeless romance or hypnotic lust by cinema, literature, and the soaps, love easily becomes another cliché.

Love has something to do with relationships, at least. In fact, it has been said that the only unconditional aspects of love are the physical, biological, psychological connections that we have literally, with our surroundings—not to mention the relationship with me, myself, and I. They're already there. We either see them, feel them, and know them or we don't. Indeed, our deepest sense of belonging is taken from the gratitude we have for, and reliance we place in, the encompassing life and minds.

These intrinsic relationships are prior to any homespun ideas we have about love as cultural commitments and social legalities. We just made those up. Innate associations with natural reality are not dependent on the times or the whims of the experts. Our given relationships with thoughts and things can't come and go—no matter our upsets, resentments, or denials. Now there's some role model for human love.

If we accept our fundamental purpose to know, experience, and identify with our body, mind, and soul, then what could possibly be more loving than to support and encourage this purpose in others? The plural is implied in the singular, so that the learning to love others is assumed in our purpose. An integrated life can't be integrated in isolation by any means or definition.

Importantly, our identity in purpose is the defining factor in our ability to love. We can relate to another's needs only to the degree that we've identified our own. We see others from where we are standing right now, accept in them that which we accept in ourselves, and express to them only that which we've had the personal pleasure. Alternatively, others can love us only to the degree that our self-love or self-loathing allows.

When loving ourselves means knowing the depths of ourselves in context with everyone else, then it's a little less selfish and a lot less flakey. A mature self-love merely honors our essential body and mind while being cognizant of the sustenance from biological ecosystems and kindred spirits.

If purpose clearly shows *why* we do everything, then love clarifies *how*. Purpose gives birth to our values, while love nurtures their thoughtful and careful enactment. Purpose is the quantity of our intention, while love is the quality of our attention. When our identity transcends the bias of biology and culture, then an emergent *quality of care* becomes the birthright of both genders.

Identification with our purposeful and loving nature allows us to give endlessly without losing and to care wholeheartedly without condition. When part of our very purpose is to value all our relationships, then kindness and compassion are spontaneous impulses. It's just how we live our lives.

The Love of Nature

> *Gravity cannot be held responsible*
> *for two people falling in love.*
> — Albert Einstein

From the beginning, subatomic social activity cooperated with self-centered individuality. Quantum particles naturally exude a mysterious complementarity. It's this long-distance communication between partner particles that exemplifies the informational wave-like nature of matter. This spooky *non-local* eavesdropping defies conventional understanding, even for the greatest minds of the century.

Chaotic *attractors* are mathematical descriptions of the informing patterns of matter. This cooperative dynamic literally grabs the self-organizing intent of matter by the privates, out from complete and utter chaos, keeping it on the straight and narrow like the clever women behind every successful man. This incredible relationship of the finest sophistication accounts for nature's precision. It's no wonder these two kids have designs on each other.

The molecular level introduces nature's physical forces. Nuclear, electromagnetic, and gravitational forces act to keep people, seas, and galaxies from flying apart. Strong nuclear forces must be the most loving, as evidenced by how unhappy and destructive they are when we try to separate them.

This joining tendency evolves in biology to create the fabulous ecosystems and symbiotic relationships throughout the rainforests and the coral reefs. Upwardly mobile, the birds and the bees provide the sensual servicing for the socially challenged flowering plants. The wind and the rain take care of any fallen seeds. The grooming behavior of chimps is nothing compared to the life cycle of the African Dung Beetle. Talk about one man's garbage...*and a little help from your friends.*

Ancient blue-green algae exhaled enough oxygen to allow the early atmosphere to support their decedents as they crawled onto the land. Mitochondria and chloroplasts were the prehistoric microbes that made the ultimate symbiotic sacrifice to become the intracellular machinery of multi-cellular plants and primates.

Outside, bacteria convert soil nutrients to be accessible for plants, while helping animals digest their food from the inside. Plants trap and store the sun's energy to photosynthesize protein, carbohydrate, and fat for the foraging animals. Animal behavior then completes the circle of life by maintaining the environment for plants to survive.

Nothing would survive at all if cooperation didn't edge out the competition. Creating complementary niches, habitats, and hierarchies are instincts that help the species endure. The timing and patterns of migration, choices of mating, and adjustment of feeding patterns are all fitting behavior for universal survival.

The same impulse that drives atoms to form molecules, stars to cluster in galaxies, and animals and plants to create ecosystems compels people to unite in communities, cities, and countries. Only the conscious awareness of our own organic nature determines how reckless or respectful we act toward life and the land.

Even predator and prey innately respect the kill as a vital balancing mechanism for the benefit of all species. Only the fearful human preys too much. Through it all, the purpose of life has evolved to sustain these relationships. The best we can do as bumbling humanoids is to watch where we're going.

Our role in the energy cycles, food chains, and the earth's atmosphere is as vital for personal purpose as are information highways. Life's fulfillment lies in the balance of being simultaneously common and unique, both partner and owner, in love and on purpose.

Sentimental tree huggers tend to elevate environmental things to living things and living things to thinking things. But again, the extreme ideologies of these Gaia-maniacs act to balance the common scientific mentality that reduces our emotions to hallucinogenic fireworks and human love to biochemistry. Either way, our longing and lusting hasn't disturbed the continuum of natural relationships that have thrived independently of what we think—so far.

The Nature of Love

> *All energy for biological processes
> ultimately comes from the sun.*
> — Biology Maxim

As the half awakened part of nature, we are the part that doubts the benevolence of these intrinsic affairs. In our mortal fear, we mistake the violence in nature for a violation of nature. Then acting in kind, our excessive killing and consuming create the very food and energy shortages and animal extinctions that we deplore. These are the symptoms of careless cross purposes and a conflicted will to live.

It's the exclusive identity with our primitive origins that allows us to misinterpret the *survival of the fittest,* thereby justifying the reduction of human behavior to animal instincts. That sentimental projection is more dangerous than the other extreme that would elevate animal emotions to human tenderness. Either way, the fittest species survive by fighting and violating as little as possible.

Communing with nature awakens a profound and primal *déjà vu.* Our ethical impulse toward the environment at large begins with the value each of us feels for our immediate and intimate surroundings.

Excessive needs for belonging and longing surface when the trust in our given supportive ties is lost. When ignored long enough, this alienation and isolation peek from under the stairs of the pervasive pain and prevailing crime we see every day.

With basic relationships forgotten and highest ones obscured, there's not much left to do but overindulge with immediate sensual gratification. Love is reduced to romantic ideals, while casual sex, exploitation, and violence are elevated to normal human instincts. A love that honors mutual purpose simultaneously seeks the fulfillment of both physical and spiritual needs.

Any truth we can grasp about love comes from whatever authenticity we bring to all our relationships. But we still have to use our brains.

The structural anatomy of our triune brain reveals the evolutionary history of all our relationships. The primitive hindbrain—the snake in all of us—relates to the physical environment. The mammalian midbrain supports the emotions and memories we use to relate to friends and family. The uniquely human neo-cortex encourages intellectual insights and higher abilities still largely unimagined. So the synaptic scaffolding for future human love is presumably already there right under our noses.

In the meantime, men are pigs. Well, if we believe that our developmental identity in love stops at the drinking age, we're sure to stumble into some boar-ish behavior. Only a soulful love can tame and refine the character of the sensual, emotional, and intellectual brain. Lower functions can be integrated up into the higher ones, making all of them more civilized. The meaning of sex and romance, marriage and community, conflict and sacrifice is clearer through the peephole of love at the level of the soul.

Love at the Level of the Body

Sex is mind over matter,
if she don't mind it don't matter.
— overheard in a bar

Our reptilian brain is responsible for the impulses and sensations necessary for feeding, mating, and defensive behavior. It's the beginning of attraction and repulsion, likes and dislikes, pain and pleasure, and basically—having relations. Love at this level, is the basic instinct of biological necessity, animal magnetism, and hot jungle sex. No thinking required.

The mystery of human attraction begins with a curious admixture of subtle aesthetics and subconscious urges—more than we might think. Symmetry, posture, and subtle movement mingle with nuances of rhythm, coordination, and manner to subliminally synchronize a compatibility factor. Aromatic pheromones mix and match with the tone, pitch, and cadence of voice to reel in certain types and throw back others.

This catch and release program undermines any predetermined shopping list that we may have imagined as our *type*. Eventually, someone or something ignites enough change in our breath, heart rate, and blood flow to make us think that we know what we're doing—or care less. If we don't honor this basic sexual chemistry within a relationship, then it's only a matter of time until it lures us away only to explode in our faces.

But again, having *good chemistry* is only as good as its greater context. This carnal knowledge is a necessary part and parcel of our organic purpose. As a tremendous biological force that ruins families, companies, and presidencies, it requires our honest attention. Just like our personality, our libido can be dulled, inflamed, or mangled enough to shirk its duties and lose its original character.

Our sexual values remain a willing slave to a self-centered purpose, in spite of our protests. The power of a shared purpose holds sex as a sacred bond, while the impotence of selfish intents can make it sinful or just plain silly. How and why we partake in the festivities determines how blessed or profane the frenzy. Our sexual experience, whether degrading or mundane, is the tell-all expose of our sexual perceptions in terms of purpose and love.

A sharpened sixth sense is merely the heightened awareness of the basic five. This subtle sensibility refines our tastes with the patience left over for any tasteless habits of friends. Childish likes and dislikes mellow from impulsive crushes and hasty revulsions to tempered desires and mature tolerances. We're easier to befriend when we're not so hot and bothered. And we're nicer to be around when we're not so fair weathered. The subtle art of seduction means we stop chasing every provocative tail of puppy love.

These are the individual sexual revelations that are needed for the communal sexual revolution to keep rolling. Music videos and motion pictures have already revealed everything they have with nothing left for the imagination. As good as it was to take sex out of the back alley, we now need to get a hold of ourselves to get over ourselves. After mastering the mechanics, we might honestly ache for the higher meaning of sex.

A physical relationship is only as satisfying and enduring as we've been able to relinquish our exclusive attachment to the lower, little brain. A higher sense of self offers a more sensible view of both sex and sexuality. From there, an all-embracing vision of lust, loving, and mating may just be what the doctor ordered to raise it out of the swamp.

Love at the Level of the Mind

Love without purpose is pure sentimentality,
purpose without love can lead to evil.
— Rollo May

Genuine caring began with packs, prides, and fraternities. The mammalian brain is the seat of the familial instincts for bonding, feeding, and defending the tribe. Human nurturing impulses now blend with these primitive responses. Together, the mixture conspires to coerce our choice in partners, confuse our desire for family and basically, trick us into getting married.

The rapture, enchantment, and ecstasy of falling in love are not to be missed, if at all possible. Romantic cloud nine and sentimental seventh heaven can't be all bad. They're good practice for being totally absorbed in the moment. Enjoy the ride, but be careful not to bet the farm on something as mindless as falling.

It's not easy to untangle the sensitive sentiments from insensitive lust, as they create similar exhilaration. The heart and the groin set a pick on the mind in order to achieve this slam dunk. And it's not hard to lose our mind, wallet, and dignity all in one three-point play.

The honeymoon eventually ends as the sex becomes lackluster, the emotional support becomes draining, and the libido goes limp. Only a warmer reception and a hardened purpose can sustain the considerate caring of higher love.

Honey, we need to talk. But communication is much more than just talking. It's a consensus about what the words really mean. *What does love mean to you? What does this relationship mean to you? Why do we bother?* When all is said and done, it's the common intention and communal attention that determines the endurance of the romantic interlude.

Compromise

Compromise means to share a promise—a shared purpose. If we feel like we're sacrificing something valuable, then we are. If our time, hobbies, or routines feel more important than our relationship, then we shouldn't make a promise that we know we can't keep. Even if we hauled away all of our precious effects, we won't really let them go. Sooner or later the wanton desire will undermine the relationship with resentment or revenge. Listen, if others have to ask for our favor, we may be compelled to *compromise* on the compromise—sort of a *faking it to make out.*

Fortunately, one need not ask and the other needn't give up anything of any real importance. In truth, it's only the excessive attachment and the distracted attention that are annoying and in need of surrendering. When the value of all the stuff in the world is not worth selling out the relationship, then the accessories naturally lose their appeal, or at least their hold.

Love isn't a competitive sport. Needless disputes over turf settle down in the warm embrace of a relationship that is going somewhere. The fading threat and resentment of competing interests means that not all outside interests need be forgotten. The added security of devoted attention allows an indulgence in external affairs, like work and hobbies, but in a new context and with priorities intact. The toys that we just can't do without become either charming, humorous, or of sentimental value. Otherwise, we'll enjoy a stoic life alone with the remote control.

Commitment

> *For helping me grow I am thankful*
> *and the wish in my kiss is that you grow*
> *and know this sweet state of bliss.*
> — Marcus Meinhold, poet

Individual interests begin to mean less when the promise of a genuine loving relationship means more. The depth of love and a couple's lifespan is a function of the heights of their purpose. But there are never any guarantees. With honest intentions, no matter what our destiny is in this crazy life, at least meaningful growth is the gift that keeps on giving.

By the time we can commit to the higher meaning of the partnership, as a third entity in itself, then dishonesty and disloyalty are not likely in our repertoire of values. Should the relationship end for legitimate reasons, we can quietly recover with our integrity intact. Because self-learning is always the goal, the time is always well spent—no regrets.

So if we still can't commit, we shouldn't. If we feel like we're giving up a part of ourselves, we are. Authentic love is characterized by a spontaneous willingness rather than a tentative resistance. Shared respect honors and listens to each other's position and availability. Cold feet are common, but not a part of genuine commitment.

It's the security and sanctity of our true identity that allows us to happily share our love and our life. We have nothing to lose once we find in our hearts that we have nothing to gain but to graciously give our love. Alternatively, by tearing down the walls in our heart, no one can tear us apart by withholding their love. A solid commitment to a meaningful relationship is a firm foundation for resolving life's inevitable pitfalls and love's boneheaded pratfalls.

Conflict

> *Let me say, with the risk of seeming ridiculous,*
> *that the true revolutionary is guided by great feelings of love.*
> — Che Guevara

Gridlock in love begins by looking for love in all the wrong places—even within wedded bliss. The fear of missing out on social and financial needs or the fervor in claiming physical and emotional needs creates a kind of a wholesale madness—the screaming, clawing, and biting usually reserved for bargain basements. Then we get home and find the flaws.

This desperation is enough to choke the life out of any good material. It's this mental scarcity that weakens all true giving and receiving, while sowing the seeds of fruitless fights. Again, the purpose of the love relationship sets the moral tone and adjusts the level of deception or outright betrayal.

Wanting too much begets resisting too much. Neurotic desires go hand-in-hand with intolerant distaste. We'll never find happiness in love without finding this give and take balance within our own heart. Admitting and overcoming our own neediness and self-critique allows us to accept any selfishness and self-deprecation of our partners. In the midst of a fight, even when it's definitely them, for our own well-being, it's always us.

When a joint account in love funds each other's concerns, there's a lot less to fight about. We trust that all our needs will be met as we meet the needs of the common bond. When the meaning of love holds the attention of both *partners-in-crime*, there is less to warrant any unwanted police action. Minor wear and tear, bumps and bruises, heal quickly when they are surrounded by a love that is mindful of the purpose of problems.

Any therapy that misses the meaning of the mêlée is just managing the details and shifting the symptoms. The highest dynamics of purpose and love are neither male nor female but characteristic of both. Attention to the similar human needs sees beyond the gender differences of the battling sexes. Granted, it may take a lifetime, but at least now the challenges are expected and even welcome in a trusting and respectful atmosphere.

Love *can* be "*never having to say you're sorry*"—depending on what we mean. In a truly loving relationship, when any harm is done, it's not intentional. We didn't mean it, didn't foresee it, or made an honest mistake. There's nothing to forgive because there's no one to blame. Of course, we can say that we're sorry if we really mean it, but the apology isn't used as a sorry excuse for getting caught.

If someone purposely hurts us, tries to get away with it, and repeats it, then an apology doesn't mean much and forgiveness is silly. We don't need an explanation and demanding one is likely a waste of time. Their character speaks loudly enough through their behavior, screaming a self-serving intent. We might take the hint. The ball is in our court. Now it's *our* character, *our* values, and *our* purpose that will determine what we decide to do and how we take care of ourselves.

The work of a relationship doesn't include second or third chances unless both parties are actually trying. But love is too complicated for others to tell us what to do or when to get out. Being honest with ourselves is even more elusive. But it never hurts to go back to the drawing board and ask each other once again—why are we here?

The need to be understood is matched only by the need to understand. Enjoying one person in the universe who knows what we're all about is not the same as the desperate need for approval. Mutual recognition is the reciprocal respect and appreciation of each other's unique self-expression. We'll recognize it when we see it.

A shared journey doesn't require having the exact same interests. The common interest is in the truth, beauty, and goodness of whatever it is that compels each person. When the competition ends, we're on the same team, designing the plays, and blocking for each other.

Love at the Level of the Soul

> *The greatest gift you can give*
> *is the quality of your attention.*
> — Richard Moss

All that unused grey matter has got to be good for something. A soul mate, like a soul purpose, is rare at best and another cliché at worst. The soul mate becomes more realistic when people relate at a profound level. We may even bump into more than one soul mate when people, in general, don't bug us so much. As our experience deepens beyond a jumble of conditioned routines and faded genes, we'll see significantly more into the soul of our spouse, who then truly becomes a significant other.

Higher reaches of soulful love open up as the purpose of the body and mind are balanced and fulfilled. Honoring lower needs bolsters the body and loosens the mind, with energy spared for higher pursuits. The *meaning* of love doesn't die when the honeymoon ends. Even the romance and the passion can endure and flourish, however modified, by embracing the higher meaning of both the sentiment and the sex.

Communion

> *Souls from the same family*
> *rarely grow up under the same roof.*
> — Source unknown

The intimate loving relationship may be the best environment in which to fulfill the furthest reaches of purpose. The people closest to us are the ones that can push our most sensitive buttons. The common hindrances in relationships suggest our most resistant issues—the buttons in the greatest need of pushing. That might account for the majority of murders by people well known to the victim—such as the spouse.

But it requires a safe haven to let down our guard, be graciously vulnerable, and unbutton our soul. Unguarded intimacy is the richest soil for cultivating the deepest love. Even deep-seated foibles and unshakeable faults become cute and quirky in light of the sense of humor that ensues with a mature love. A quiet communion develops in the certainty of deeply shared values. *You just know.*

It's this communal purpose that nurtures a unique and abiding love. When we're not married to the finite differences, we're free to court the infinite similarities. Rather than tolerating the cultural stereotypes, we're able to soar above them. The object of our affection becomes a subject of our fullest attention. When love is who we are, it's also how we live our lives.

The unadulterated work of true love is the greatest human challenge. It's more interesting and rewarding than sacrifice, compromise, and agreeing to disagree. Conflicts are constructive and the pain is worthwhile when accepted and expected as a means to a fairy tale ending. We'll enjoy new and improved "*discussions*" each year, not nearly as disheartening and draining as decades of the same useless arguments.

Selfish behavior is reconciled and rectified in the light of a certain higher Self-ishness. We'll know the difference because when our actions hurt everyone in the long run, including ourselves, they're driven by fear and insecurity. When we lovingly take the time for self-respecting care that helps one and all, now and forever, then it's not a problem—it's love.

Compassion

> *All you need is love, but love is not enough.*
> *It depends on what you mean.*
> — Gary Ratson

Compassion means to "*suffer with*" someone. We ease the pain of others by sharing in it. Empathy asks us to walk in another's shoes, while compassion mandates that we first hike a little bit in our own. Passionately tackling our own obstacles and striving for our own purpose gives us the strength and the wherewithal to seriously relate to the struggle of others. We don't have to *do* anything in particular to provide genuine comfort or consolation. We just need to be there as a benevolent presence.

Presence means *"to be"* and as a loving presence we're honestly being ourselves, reminding others to trust in their own healing heart. It's more than our welcoming smile, warm eyes, gentle movements, and sincere tone of voice that warms another's heart. These are manifestations of the primary loving awareness that puts people at ease, makes them feel at home, and assures them that someone cares. When an average looking person is surprisingly radiant or a flawless face comes across as cold and callous, it reminds us something about loving presence.

Loving Presence

> *That which comes from the heart,*
> *speaks to the heart.*
> — Jewish sage

A loving presence fills a room just as a commanding presence issues forth from a revered authority. Lighting up a room, the loving being creates an instant attraction and a rapport that is palpable, consensual, and memorable. The allure and charisma about these people is unarguable. The hospitable ambience is directly felt as a quickening in all subtle senses. Their home, the décor, and all the furnishings are bestowed with the force of their radiant character.

The kindness, graciousness, and peacefulness in the presence of such a person are as dramatic as the atmosphere in a holy shrine or sacred event. Their total acceptance and focused concern can be the most touching and memorable moment of our lives. If we knew how they did it and that it was possible, we might strive to become like that ourselves.

Most of us are probably more familiar with the opposite. Nasty individuals can fill a room with a dark and intimidating coldness. The mean-spirited tension can be cut with a knife. It's downright chilling. Chances are they don't believe in anything spiritual and it's *that* vacuum that they so effectively use to suck the soul right out of a room, along with the light and the heat.

Whatever it is, a loving presence has an overwhelming influence on young minds for learning and for healing. What children, students, and patients need most from us cannot be taught. They need us to be who we really are.

The Meaning of Children

> *The power is at the beginning.*
> — Lao Tzu

Child development is a complicated and unique mix of culture, family, genetics, and personal experience. As parents, we would like to have a child grow up to be principled, smart, and happy. But strangely enough, they want to be like us.

It's this rather mindless biological attachment that makes them so vulnerable. The first few weeks, months, and years are more precious and precarious for the unfolding persona than is commonly realized. This is the time when a loving influence orchestrates the neurological network and lays the emotional groundwork that protects the future teenager from the scourge of society's ills.

Even before birth, the fetal stress response is up and running with the mother's perceptions, relationships, and household conditions. Any parental fighting or fleeing is felt at the heart of the womb, shunting prenatal blood from vital brain and body centers to potentially stunt the loving and learning character of the growing personality.

Newborns have an instinctive trust of their environment, as if it revolved around them. The sooner their faith in the surroundings is shattered, the harder it is to consciously recoup later on—the crux of the adult healing process. Of course, it's this same direct knowing that gives healthy parents the genteel awareness of their tremendous opportunity and influence over the fragile young psyche.

Traumatic at best, the speed of the child's changing world is always challenging, no matter how righteous the parents. Continuous navigation of new worlds requires some major global positioning. That's the role of the parents. The love and security of *home sweet home* creates a numinous ambience to act as a psychic grid, guiding and orientating the developing mind.

It's no surprise that the greatest blocks to future development would come at the time when growth and learning are at their peak. The biggest advances in life happen in the first two years and do not requiring any teaching—muscular coordination and language. That's walking and talking. Following our lead, children run and ask questions to satisfy their own emotional curiosity. That's how normal growth and development happen before self-consciousness allows the doubts, fears, and tantrums to kick in. These they learn from us.

It follows that the most good and the most evil is perpetrated at the same sacred time. Those in intimate positions, trusted to do the most good, are in the position to do the most harm—the doctor, teacher, clergy, and the parents. When adult ignorance meets infant innocence, big-time harm is often inflicted.

This breach of trust by the elders is not an intellectual gap as much as a crack in their instinctive shell and a loss of faith in spontaneous growth and healing. Any weakened judgment of what is best for the child often cries out from a heartbroken version of love and purpose. The kid's world is at the mercy of their mentor's world and it can be a world of hurt.

But even everyday misunderstandings create torment, shame, and confusion in the innocent young mind. The routine hurts and humiliations of childhood relegate a good portion of the promising persona into the self-deprecating shadow that kids drag behind them to school each day. It's not necessarily anything the parents did. It's just how they are.

What are neurotic, psychotic, or socio-pathic disorders if not different degrees of denial and obsession—the attachments and aversions of stunted and mangled personalities? No matter the theories and statistics of disordered personas, the essential identity is lost, the view of Self is diminished, and the perception of life is distorted. Nobody is just born like that.

Character, integrity, and ethics emerge like all psychological traits in an emotionally safe environment. Even if food, clothing, and shelter are a hardship, the loving presence of the parents secures the nurturing and nourishing support. The most meaningful values are imparted by mom and dad's manner of speaking and acting with each other, friends, and neighbors. The clearest message comes from their honest intentions rather than their specific circumstances or college degrees. The greatest thing for children is a playground born of purpose that encourages the love for learning.

So you still want to have a baby? The question to ask then is, *"What are the biological, emotional, and spiritual reasons for creating a person?"* It's only a cute little bundle of joy for a few months. Maternal instincts, emotional needs, and family legacy just don't cut it for very long. Who is supposed to carry whom? This sovereign entity, this whole new person, cannot be unfairly burdened with the parent's unmet needs.

With balanced priorities, parents will trust that satisfying their lesser needs will be a joyful side effect of committing to the vital needs of the new addition. The reasons for having a baby plant the seeds for a lifelong relationship. Much of the tension between adult children and parents goes back to these earliest conceptions of purpose. Empty-nesters might well work harder *right now* to bridge any conflict with a grown child if their ancient intentions still held any water. *He's still your forty-year-old handful.*

The most enduring reason for anything is the reason that never dies—sharing the wealth of love and purpose. The kid may actually call home once in a while.

Learning

*When motivated by fear
all one remembers is the fear.*
— Rabbi Schneerson

Teachers are always demanding our undivided attention. Natural curiosity and the love of learning don't fade away by grade school. They're either standing outside the principal's office or they're grounded. The ordinary deficits of attention symbolize a common deficiency of thought and care in familial and cultural conditioning. The innate quest for the knowledge is ironically stifled by our own taboos.

Love means we have to be interested enough to pay attention and remember what people say. That's the same attention span required for learning. Loving and learning both insist on clear reception and precise retention. But the toddler's snoopiness and puppy love for learning often gets hushed and swatted away, only to return from the dead as a monstrous apathy and absent-mindedness that now frightens the parents and stifles the teachers.

The everyday learning deficit is nothing less than a fearful disorder of love and purpose. Granted, sometimes it's something more than that. But it's not necessary to be an intellectual giant to succeed in grade school. Those early grades are not any tougher than learning a mother's tongue—and the students have already done that. Besides the mindless conditioning of television and video games, attention and curiosity are mistakenly arrested when the parents are guilty of repeatedly minimizing the kids' honest inquiries.

Children need to know that their intuitions and instincts are valid and valued. They identify strongly with their timid ideas, so their esteem can be shot down with the wave of a hand—and with that, their tentative plans for the future. Their little insights are the seeds of all branching knowledge that parents could do well to recall. It's not a matter of parents having all the right answers but of carefully questioning their own intentions.

Discipline

> *Obeying from love is better than to obey from fear.*
> — Rabbi Solomon Ben Issac

Discipline comes from the word *"disciple"*—the follower of an exemplar. Punishments that cultivate purpose and nurture love make more sense to kids than those designed to break their will. They know that forcing a spontaneous behavior is meaningless.

The value of any childhood punishment depends on how much it honors the kid's intention and offers instruction. Meaningless punishment promotes meaningless behavior. It then fosters resentment, disrespect, and revenge that establish the merry-go-round of crime and punishment.

The judgment of good or bad begins in the parent's rushed and inconvenienced perception. Initially without any bad intentions, a child is left utterly confused by the threatening reprimands it receives from a well-meaning guardian. Only as parents appreciate the importance of youthful curiosity will they provide the safe environment for it to flourish.

When expected to perform beyond their age and ability, children come off looking bad in the eyes of those parents who unwittingly create the conditions to fail. By the time the kid is annoying the parents on purpose, the little rascal is likely getting back at the folks in the only way he knows, for something they don't even know they did—like waving the youngster off while they were busy.

Children can't be expected to behave like angels while witnessing their support network being threatened by silences, arguments, or outright fights. We don't need to be super-moms and dads. We just need to know what we're doing and why. Even the gender roles we impose with pinks and blues can inhibit the fullest expression of the early personality. Human traits and behaviors, like purpose and love, aren't distinguished by colors presumed to be masculine or feminine.

For the punishment to fit the crime, it should be as honest as the crime. When little ones are *sentenced* to read a book, do some chores, or give away toys to sick kids, then their attention is focused on something sensible rather than something unreasonable. The time spent creating imaginative punishments impresses the child with genuine caring and learning values.

In the stressful haste of busy lives, childhood is reduced to spankings, time-outs, and withholding love. Reward and punishment, like threats and bribes, teach our most recent values. The message is that being good must be forced, boring, and difficult. Everything is for sale at the right price. When cartoon logos and commercial endorsements are used to entice kids to brush their teeth and wash their hands, the eventual man-child has never learnt to do anything simply because it needs doing.

Enforcing behavior means we don't have to mean anything that we do in life. Demanding respect is as useless as asking for a commitment. It's like threatening someone to love us, then bribing them to mean it. Using pain and pleasure to induce goodness and truth is treating children like reptiles and expecting them to behave like mammals. Sort of.

Public service warnings of death and disease from drugs, alcohol, and junk food have proven that fear is never a good motivator. When it is the motivating factor, the ingrained fear can be worse than the behavior. Doing anything out of fear is short lived and ineffective, while living in fear is the worst vice we can have. But we can't really use love to motivate someone until we know the value of it first hand.

These days, rewards are more harmful than the punishments. The treats, toys, and videos that stymie curiosity, imagination, and physical activity are worse than taking these *privileges* away because their harm is so casually denied. The message that gets through is that working hard must also be forced, boring, and difficult. Afterwards, we can reward ourselves with some mindless fun to forget about our day. Sounds like the mantra of everyone down at the pub, doesn't it?

Presumptions of a child's best interests are limited to one's version of "*best.*" What seems best for others is judged only at the depth of our own experience and identity in purpose. Finding the best of the best, or at least better and better, means continually confronting our own painful experiences so as not to repeat or project them on others.

But the little charmers love us in spite of ourselves. They remind us that somewhere inside we're still kind of loveable. They try to be good for us, even if it means cheating to do it because they want us to be happy. To the extent we actually help others and take care of our things, the kid may still idolize us when she's twenty-five, because it makes sense. Sensing our ways, they'll learn to listen to their own heart and a natural conscience will guide their behavior just fine.

Mostly though, as parents we love our kids too much, help them too much, and hold on too tightly. We're afraid for them to suffer even the necessary pain and disappointments inherent in normal growth. Realizing how we engender children's fears and avoidance through our own insecurity and denial is a good place to start for family growth and healing.

When everyone on the last place team receives a trophy, the lessons of sport are severely lessened. Until we suffer our own passion to reap the hard-won rewards, the true meaning of compassion often gets past us. The tennis great Arthur Ashe spoke of *loving loosely* by allowing his children to make their mistakes and earn their lessons. It requires the full strength of our character to teach our children about theirs.

Highly prized actions speak louder than words, but everything we say and do pales in comparison to the loving environment created by our mere presence. The love or fear that helps or harms early child development is a function of the combined parental identity. Children are most nourished by the silent character, values, and integrity of the parental union, the by-products of mutual purpose.

So then of course, there are no absolute rules for parenting. Any enduring guidelines are limited by the care and intent with which they're enacted. The child's basic needs are hopefully a given. But meeting all of a youngster's needs requires the presence of a safe, loving, and learning atmosphere—then for us to get out of their way.

Lovin' Good Vibrations

> *Love does not consist of gazing at each other*
> *but in looking outward together in the same direction.*
> — de Saint Exupery Antoine

Meaningful love is a profound factor in longevity and health. The sense of separateness and alienation creates an illusory disconnect from intrinsic relationships in life. The subsequent fear and loneliness hinders learning, development, and possibilities. Choices and behaviors that are antagonistic to health are a consequence of the carelessness and thoughtlessness of a lost inner love.

Without a profound identity in higher love, we easily become another statistic. Our self-worth dies along with the death of a spouse if we're too attached, and the body often follows suit within the year. The more common nagging-to-death comes under another category.

The quality of our lives is determined by the nature of all our relationships—which also add to the quantity of our lives. The will to live is nothing if not the commitment and loyalty to the value of life. The *will to love* that sustains us during times of bitter loss is the next of kin to the will to live.

Our present level of awareness in love has a corresponding physiology that reflects the balance of desires and aversions, inner accord or discord. Any imbalances can grow into attachments and rejections that encourage the various addictions and afflictions to further compound the biological heartache.

We can't hurry love and it's hard to measure. It doesn't show up in the blood work; we can't control for it or rule it out. Yet it might just account for the confounding evidence in the studies and statistics. Science says that married people live longer, but surely the legal parchment itself is not life-giving. Rather, the answers on the surveys are *secondary* expressions of a primary loving awareness in the couples that keep it together—alive and well.

How and why we're divorced, single, or bicoastal has more physiological effects than any legalities, demographics, and unique circumstances. Love and purpose manifest themselves biochemically no matter the household arrangements. While soaring divorce rates are unnerving, they partly reflect a realization that previous generations weren't free to act on—the meaningless relationship.

As we get cozy with an ultimate level of love, we develop an intimate trust in our own emotional and biological healing milieu. The greater our sense of universal belonging, the more time we'll save dreaming and hoping for extraterrestrial saviors.

By any definition, what could be more loving than seeking the highest intentions and developing the finest attention? Purpose channels our emotions and sustains intimacy, while love keeps our purpose on track. Any distinctions between love and purpose eventually blur. Together they establish just how well we respond to life's many challenges. Experiencing true love and authentic purpose clearly remains our primary responsibility—and our original duty.

* * *

Inferring Responsibility

As a kid, I already wanted to be a good person, someday. I didn't need any goofy inducements or threats. I could get that anywhere. I needed something else. Yet for the most part, I thought I had to listen to the adults if only because they had the experience. The worst thing I ever did was stay up past my bedtime. I argued with my parents that my neighbor was allowed to learn for himself that staying up as late as he wanted wasn't the greatest thing in the world.

By high school, my success or failure in life felt like it could go either way. I had no idea how to influence my fifty-fifty chance of being any kind of a hero or a complete waste of space. Going to university was a no-brainer. I had nowhere else to go. But I envied those who did.

Days of relative calm alternated with weeks of frustration and despair. I wanted to have some say in my ultimate fate, but I just couldn't get good information. I knew I saw things a little differently than other people, but that I couldn't be entirely wrong. I just couldn't shake my inner voice that implied I would take the fall for a society that had it upside down and backwards. No, if my life was going to suck, it's because I sucked. Life itself was fine.

It seemed to me that if you need to be told not to murder people, maybe it won't help very much. My interpretation of the Ten Commandments was that this is how normal grown-ups behave. If you grow up, you will too. In the meantime, try not to hurt people. Yet, the brash and the balls of the criminal element intrigued me as much as the extraordinary behavior of nicer folks. I had little in common with these street toughs, but they also seemed to know something I didn't.

Any inkling I had for right or wrong came through my sixth sense for creepiness. The only place we could play pinball was in sleazy downtown arcades, dumps full of peep shows, girly magazines, tattoos, piercings, smoking, drugs, and the ne'er-do-wells who enjoyed that stuff. Later on, I didn't need to know anything about morality to recognize the same seediness behind the schemes, the sex shows, and the creeps in the glitzy glamour of Las Vegas. Even the phony façades of Disneyland seemed like a Vegas prep school to me. I guess I wasn't a pile of fun, but I couldn't wash away the memory of those dirty arcades.

"I've used up all my sick days, so I'm calling in dead!" I was shocked to learn that people get paid when they don't work, take holidays, and get sick or injured. I never had that job. Then I heard about people banking sick days to add onto vacation time, working just enough to collect unemployment insurance—and my favorite—milking their injuries for workers' compensation. It all looked like the same creepiness factor to me. These goof-offs weren't even trying.

Parents would always plead with celebrities and athletes to behave themselves because they were role models for little Johnny. Now, I never really idolized anyone, but it seemed to me that I should desire to be like someone worthy of emulating, not just someone pretending because my mom asked them to. People screw up all the time. I'll choose another hero, so don't do me any favors. I can think for myself. Maybe I'll admire the achievement rather than the person. Parents forget their own conflicting scolds, like "Would you jump off a bridge if your friends jumped off a bridge...?" Hey, which is it going to be? Either I'm supposed to follow, or I'm not supposed to follow.

People accomplish more incredible things in the worst of possible circumstances than I can even imagine at the best of times. How do I become like that guy? What does she know that I don't? And why can't I just do it now before some tragedy hits? I was always so moved and curiously envious of permanently injured and disabled people who accomplished great things and became great leaders.

Nelson Mandela led a nation while flourishing in prison for twenty-seven years. Viktor Frankl re-wrote Man's Search for Meaning in a POW camp—on toilet paper. Stephen Hawking leads theoretical physicists while being virtually paralyzed. Christopher Reeve lives and leads heroically with quadriplegia. Surely, it doesn't make sense for me to need that kind of grief before I get off the couch. I routinely imagined myself in these worst-case scenarios, and wondered how I would hold up, and if some punk would think it was neat.

Of course, it was just as fascinating to read about the serial killers, the cannibals, and the terrorists. I was always intrigued with all the extremists, the zealots, the alien abductees, and the rest of the crazies—I mean, what got into these people?

I thought a lot about death. But nobody else wanted to talk about it. It seemed to me that when it's imminent, it's too stressful and too late to bother.

At funerals, I really wanted to get into a deep discussion about death and dying, but people were always busy eating. So instead, I enjoyed reading about near-death experiences, channeling and psychic phenomena, and the unexplained wonders of the world. I didn't care about seeing the light, bending spoons, or building pyramids—I just wanted to hear what others thought about living and dying right now. Never mind reincarnation—I couldn't believe I was born this time.

I thought a lot about suicide. Oh, not for me. But it's not uncommon and I tried to imagine how bad life has to feel when the fear of living becomes greater than the fear of killing yourself. I wondered what complete and utter hopelessness feels like—and how far away it is from how my life felt. Somehow, the extreme despair of others made me think how easy I had it and encouraged me to dream about living a better life than I had been. Far from morbid, I knew early on that I learned more from grief than from fun.

But I was always more of a watcher than a doer. So this better-life thing is going to take some time. For sure, I knew that I would spend the first half of my life figuring out what the hell I'm doing. I won't let myself regret it—I simply had no other way. If there is a second half, I can see myself being a good old-guy. Yes, an old soul, imparting timeless wisdom to family and friends, if I have any left by then.

The Meaning of Responsibility

*A man with a why to live for
can handle almost any how.*
— Viktor Frankl

Responsibility has that imposing, parental tone of a chore to be done, a rule to be followed, a schedule to meet, or a penalty to be served. *Sit up straight, do your homework, stop touching yourself, and for God's sake, behave.* Ouch! Society and our boss, like our parents before, don't care whether we mean it or not. Just do it.

But what about the earnest soul who cares for his family, pays his taxes, and obeys the traffic signals to live a life of quiet desperation and not-so-quiet exasperation? Rules and regulations are attempts to protect the public's interest at large. On the other hand, an individual's best interests are served by the motivation and care that inspires his or her obligations and commitments to others. That's purpose and that's love. Been there, done that. Responsibility to society, humanity, and the environment is an inevitable side effect of a loving purpose.

The laws of the land never healed anyone. The legal wizards that come up with that stuff aren't any healthier or more law abiding than anyone else. Laws barely mean anything if the masses are merely suppressing a murderous rage. In any event, we can still do whatever we want—once.

Just like medicine, the law gives us a false sense of security. Neither remedial remedy can be relied upon for an individual's safety, and certainly don't guarantee compliance or well-being. Like a policing paternal threat, the long arm of the law only enforces the *appearance* of good intentions—for the time being.

In fact, the *spirit of the law* does more to shape behavior than the word of law. The meaning of the law already reflects the cultural intent and the community of care, and thus needs no enforcement. These collective inner rules exist prior to the written regulations. The subsequent *social ambience* of a lawful society continues to incite rightful behavior between the lines of the law. It's a chicken and egg thing, where the legal seeds are first laid down within the citizens' increasingly rich imagination to be hatched later in the right political climate.

The law is like advice—good people don't need it, ignorant people won't heed it. We *are* above the law, or at least ahead of it when our added perception of right and wrong helped create the credo. Then our behavior smoothly sides with our leading values and it just looks like we're following the social guidelines.

Those reading this book are probably not the one's looting stores during a riot. But the reasons we don't cheat, steal, or kill has little to do with the legalities or penalties. Our morality, civility, and humanity are a willful and careful response to our perceived value of life and the property of others. Any irresponsibility we enjoy is a function of exaggerated or denied personal needs—the original legislative body.

As a society, when the majority of us experience a little more of our own humanity, our laws naturally become a little more humane—and we become humanitarians. Now it's true that excruciating bureaucracies often force the outspoken few to break the real crusty laws, but civilization in general marches to the civility of the people. Protests and demonstrations are often needed as wake up calls to the old thinking behind really tired laws. But ultimately, the politicos lay in wait for the masses to change their stripes.

If purpose is *why* and love is *how* we live our lives, then responsibility is *what* we actually do. Healthy responsibility is prior to policy and policing, out in front of codes of conduct. Our response to life will only be as thoughtful and valuable as our combined identity in purpose and love.

Any intentions to align our choices and behaviors with the tenets of religion, city hall, or our parents are forever entwined with the knee-jerk responses of our tightly wound personality. If this is as good as we get, at least we mean it. Granted, we should try to live beyond our means, looking good and acting right, but it becomes exhausting. The high cost of this phony baloney takes the gusto out of recovering from any immediate fumbles.

Responsibility is an evolving process of responding to life, by request. We can pay now with love and attention or we can pay later with compounding interest and liability.

The Nature of Responsibility

Of course, we've all heard *"Where there's a will, there's a way."* But realize that purpose is the *will* and responsibility is the *way*. Responsibility is our *ability to respond*. It's our eagerness to confront life's obstacles, challenges, and crises. Secure in the knowledge that all variety of heartache is beneficial for rising above our current limitations, we'll make the most out of all sorts of pain.

Dreadful experiences are natural signs of life. We're not gluttons for punishment to admit that failure breeds more learning than success or that suffering inspires more creativity than creature comforts. The key to this distinction is in knowing which grief is unavoidable and legitimate and which is homespun and gratuitous. Those with the keenest sense of responsibility take on supportive roles in situations that might appear beyond their jurisdiction. But these people know intuitively that for all intents and purposes, there's always something they can do.

People who automatically see challenge as an opportunity, the glass as half full, and enjoy making lemonade are not reciting clichés, repeating mantras, or invoking visualizations. They actually live this way. As their identity transcended the confines of body and personality type, they attained a position of power—a position to powerfully influence their physical, emotional, and social experience.

Responsibility taps into this authentic inner power. It's a further refinement of the power gained through the strength of our character. Courage comes from the French word *cour*, meaning heart. The courage to face our fears with all our heart comes from the heartfelt strength of a powerfully-built identity. It's the sure-fire way to declare ownership of our experiences, take stewardship over our environment, and attain authorship over our destiny—without overstating it.

The subtle power of responsibility is more profound and enduring than the obvious power of money, prestige, or position. In fact, it's this unique clout that helps us achieve a reasonable financial punch and then defend it with a clear conscience. The same personal affluence saves us when we get downsized, seized by our assets, or relegated to the bargain bin. We simply handle it like a professional person.

The real defiant ones brush against the cold harshness of reality, against all odds, with no holds barred, taking all comers, to boldly go where.... anyway, they recognize life's struggles for all they're worth, using everything they have to make the misery mean something. The triumph of the human spirit is always right here for anyone who cares to notice it.

Responsibility now makes sense for health. It puts the brakes on the helplessness that drives the entitlement gravy train. It snuffs out the greed and vengeance that fuels the litigiousness fires. And it tears the flags of powerlessness off the victim-hood bandwagon. Importantly, responsibility heals these weaknesses at the source of their fury with the help, hope, and power that come from a truly open heart.

Confronting conflict early doesn't mean we avoid all problems. It means we graciously accept the necessary plights as eventualities and opportunities, thereby *not making them worse*. Then we prevent the creation and inflammation of uncalled for troubles—which are much more common. The spiritual warrior has the extrasensory ammunition and paranormal resources to pay in advance.

Asking *why bad things happen to good people* is, with all due respect, a childish holdover from our reward-punishment school-days internment. It's a poor question. Life seems fair or unfair only when we misjudge the meaning of good and bad. Comfort and solace in difficult times requires the particular power to discern the difference, and the similarities. Things are never as bad as they seem but neither are they as great as we might have imagined once we let go of excessive pessimism or mislaid romanticism.

Notice too, that angry criminals can languish in jail until a ripe old age, while the most kindhearted souls may bear unbearable grief only to suffer an early demise. For better *and* worse, life is going happen. It behooves us to take our heads out of the sand and seriously wrap our brains around this reality. The French know, *c'est la vie*.

Good things are agreeable only because bad things are so disagreeable. Pleasure gets its reputation due to pain's ill repute, while beauty is attractive since ugliness is so repulsive. Finally, our appreciation of life ironically grows with our appreciation of death. This old poetic wisdom urges us to face our rollercoaster existence with its curves and swerves of happiness and sadness—accepting life just as it is.

Interestingly, we create just as many conflicts and symptoms with how and why we respond to the *good* things in our lives—like friends and family—as we do with the bad things. *So count your blessings—everything's relative.*

There's something to be said for going with the flow and riding the rhythms of life's ups and downs. The inconvenient disaster that forces us to take a break, reassess our situation, and come up with ideas we otherwise wouldn't, can turn adversity into the best thing that ever happened. These rather rude awakenings remind us just how literally we took our schooling in pursuing happiness by avoiding sadness.

Adam and Eve taught us that the higher consciousness of good and evil does not come without the garden variety wake-up call. In sickness and in health, our necessary evils need to be taken, and taken seriously.

We could decide that goodness will define those experiences that foster the highest reaches of purpose and love. And of course, it does. Then by default, we might choose to see bad things as a reminder that someone has forgotten about purpose and love. Not a bad deal either way. The only alternative is to live like most of us live right now—squeezing the living daylights out of good and bad alike.

With this in mind, being mindful of intermittent intrusions is more conducive to healing than seeking the mindless perpetual pleasure we daydream about while thumbing through the travel section. Clinging to the ledge of the good life and denying all fears of aging and death, we forget that our immortality lives in the meaning that we milk from the tough times.

It's this hard-wired, grace-under-fire gratitude for life that serves to trigger more mature questions. *Why don't bad things happen more often* and *why not me?* Ever noticed that people who live like this seem to attract less hardship? Or maybe because they handle problems quickly and quietly, it just appears that way.

Many people think that human beings never change because the oldest crimes indeed persist like the oldest professions. We still travel along the same tortuous and traumatic developmental path and can get bumped off at any time. But laws, like security techniques, are obliged to keep up with increasing criminal ingenuity—the crimes are evolving along with the criminals. Ultimately, legal and illegal will be synonymous with healthy and unhealthy. Then the law will join the ultimate medicine and the original religion in healing our global amnesia of love and purpose.

The Responsibility of Nature

> *You can't solve a problem*
> *from the same level that created it.*
> — Albert Einstein

The spontaneous responses in nature form the basis of human responsibility that we find easier said than done. But red army ants don't give a second thought to rebuilding a whole civilization after little Johnny drags his shovel through it.

It's silly to speak of *matter* as consciously making choices. Yet, particulate matter does seem to interact, adapt, and change its expression in the presence of various technologies. The *wavicle* nature of subatomic bits tunes into such nosy neighbors, politely displaying what they want to see. Existence has been officially deemed a participatory event for everyone who's invited—R.S.V.P.

In order to fulfill their designs, things are required to hold their ground and sustain their character to the best of their ability. Exerting a defiant independence, subatomic information and energy wields a self-referring quality. This acts as an internal memo from its own self-organizing files to stay the course and to disregard any Monday morning quarterbacking. This unyielding subatomic bump and grind also provides the hard rock reality that makes it so tricky to walk through walls.

Natural disasters have something to do with the Pauli Exclusion Principle that states, *"No two particles can occupy the same space."* They needed a principle for that? Nevertheless, matter responds with exploding nebula, volcanoes, earthquakes, and the rest to carve out the galaxies, mountain ranges, and our own corner lot.

These resistive dynamics, allied with the cooperative and ordering principles, compelled all *living* things to take their place and take a stand. Plants powered against the gravitational pull and stumbled upon wooden trunks. Birds rolled the dice to partner up to the falling sky with feathered wings. Vertebrates fell ass backwards into bony skeletons and decided to stand up for themselves. Responsibility in biology is nicely demonstrated as the naturally selecting force of evolution where species and the environment co-resist and co-respond to further co-pilot evolutionary chance and necessity.

The laws of nature predict general decay, deterioration, and disorder while biological law defiantly counters with specific development, healing, and survival. The apparent "*struggle for existence*" oddly parallels the harmonizing design of natural relationships—something like "*struggle locally, commune globally.*"

The insecurity of our self-imposed exile from nature's garden causes us to be overly defensive and compulsively resistant. So we destroy more than we create, consume more than we commit, and compete more than we cooperate. That's irresponsible. It's purpose without love.

We usually interpret *survival of the fittest* to mean genetically fit, thereby reducing ourselves to some kind of inbred selfish creatures. We tend to overlook the mental toughness we used to survive primitive life and ignore the spiritual finesse that will keep us flourishing. Spiritual responsibility is the strongest link in the future of the *great chain of becoming*—the evolving continuum of existence.

Responsibility at the Level of the Body

The art of living lies less in eliminating troubles
than in growing with them.
— Bernard Baruch

The likelihood of learning increases with the magnitude of misfortune. Unfortunately, it takes a good war, a large military operation, or a police action to inspire the most sophisticated technologies and humane democracies. Similarly, the motivation behind leading medical research and advances is stirred by disease, distress, and death. Luckily for us, the renegade ideas that shape extreme sports also trickle down to the local outdoors stores providing the masses with all that really neat gear.

By responding with our undivided attention to natural disasters, inexplicable suffering, and inevitable mistakes, we advance to the next level of civilized sorrow. With the steadfast intention to honor our role in the inescapable ruin, we achieve a greater acumen for avoiding senseless despair.

The degree and duration of our pain and suffering is largely determined by how we bear our burdens. Damage and discomfort are prolonged and exaggerated by fear and avoidance. All symptoms are overcome sooner with care and attention. With the trust in our innate biological will and a reliance on our vast emotional resources, we defuse the denial that hinders all healing.

It helps to imagine symptoms as signs toward our best intentions and signals en route to our true love interests. These painful inferences are like intimate friends, nudging, prodding, and pushing the buttons we can't conceal any longer. Ignoring early warning signs actually creates most of the ordinary nuisances and slows our response time to the extraordinary predicaments. The mature handling of early distress is simply the loving expression of a responsible identity.

Most day-to-day dread is created by our own mistaken ideas and impulsive reflexes. This *neurotic* suffering needlessly drains energy away from any higher pursuits. It also revs up the resistance for avoiding pressing issues, leaving mundane molehills to become mountainous.

Responsibility is not about thinking ourselves well or forcing our will. Rather, it's the recognition that any further force amounts to resisting a resistance that is already there. If we agree that symptoms represent defenses and repairs that are already impeded, then continued interference is redundant and harmful.

During illness, the original battle of good and evil is being waged in our body. The argument between likes and dislikes becomes enraged to desperation and disgust. An even worse battle erupts if we continue to respond with further aggression or apathy. To declare a cease fire means we finally stop fanning the flames. By putting down our worry-worn weaponry and tattered emotional defenses, we admit that we're making a mess. We're not magically *creating* healing but rather trusting and allowing the miracle of normal healing to proceed—often with the courage to do nothing.

The power of attention alone can release a muscular tension or ease an emotional strain. We can't realize just how much we make things worse until we have the experience of making them a lot better. This attention to detail can literally fine-tune the perception of color, contrast, and comfort of any painful contraction. Simply exerting our presence on the situation is the conscious witnessing that allows us to gain some perspective, release our intellectual grip, and let down our guard.

Simultaneously, by acknowledging the body parts that are still comfy and by noticing any pleasing immediate surroundings, we lighten the load. When consumed by a knowing trust that things do get better, there's little reason to beat ourselves up. Now, as we stop identifying with our disease, disfigurement, or damaging deeds, these hardships begin to fall under some semblance of control.

Why suppress, dull, and avoid when we might experiment and experience the meaning of the unfortunate circumstances, now in a controllable fashion. It only seems a morbid obsession from the exiled view as our own worst enemy. Rather, morbidity flourishes and is obviously entertained by the denial of responsibility.

Passion means *to suffer*, referring to the valid struggle in pursuit of a loving purpose. Unavoidable annoyance and irritation is a natural aspect of getting to know our physical selves. This experience builds our strength for *com*-passion while enlivening our contagious healing radiance.

None of this precludes us from taking the edge off with a little help from our generic friends. But how and why we imbibe or prescribe determines the ultimate value of any therapy. The widespread overuse, misuse, and abuse of treatment come from our fearful conditioning, mistaken mistrust, and ignorance of mental tools and techniques. At best, the side effects are an unrelenting encore of symptoms, the painful reminder of a neurotic déjà view.

Symptoms are *symbols* that suggest something more. A not-so-subtle hint, they're a call to the multiple influences and imbalances from within and without. Like all truths, symptoms never exist in isolation. Their multi-factorial nature alludes to their biological, emotional, and cultural meaning. When symptoms are perceived as meaningless, then so is the treatment, with the patient coming in third.

Recall that responsibility is also a balance of power. The doctor, teacher, politician, and parents take theirs. We take ours. If *unnatural* guilt or blame escalates, our options seem to shrink to one hundred percent victim or crime. This narrow view leads to a tapered quest for easy answers. Then, we confidently scapegoat the genes, the germs, the parents, or the gods as the various studies come and go. Alternatively, the *natural* guilt of a healthy conscience readily reminds us that we indeed know better.

Paternalistic medicine, like an overbearing religion, dishonors our role by misunderstanding the meaning of wholeness and holiness. Denying our responsibility devalues our purpose, demoralizes our behavior, and stymies the doctor-patient relationship. The fear of missing something leads to the anxiety of doing nothing and the foible of overdoing everything. The multiple doctors of elderly patients have little time to sort out the sundry side effects of their many drug cocktails that are hardly on the side.

We all know what happens when people are not invited to attend their own healing. Uncle Buck doesn't know the name of his diseases or his medications, often mixing up meds and mistaking the doses. Aunt Fanny's fearful ignorance leaves her noncompliant, yet she hoards the leftover pills with copious amounts of over-the-counter concoctions, just for good measure. When health is reduced to a commodity, we can buy, sell, and trade it around the condo. Not a very informed consensus.

Treatment that is motivated by fear inevitably makes things worse. The massive hysteria and singular blame of normal bacteria allows companies to load hygiene and household products with needless antibiotics. Meanwhile, anxious mothers coerce their pediatricians to over-prescribe for baby's every little sniffle. Antibiotic resistance is modern medicine's monster—an evil genie that decades of fear-mongering haven't been able to put back in the bottle.

Too little responsibility and too much love inevitably slow things up. Injured workers often never return to work, even without intentional secondary gain. With no love lost at work and the monetary benefits of worker's compensation, a fledgling healing motive can easily be sidetracked by drug or alcohol abuse. Alternatively, seriously injured professional athletes are back on the playing field in no time when motivated by fame, pride, and mega-bucks. That's big-time responsibility, albeit mixed with the potent steroids and pain pills.

These days, going to a hospital is like going to the mall. We can browse the boutiques, smoking sections, and fast-food kiosks awaiting our small bowel follow-through. These health care values, like the institutions themselves, are too sick to provide a genuine healing environment and too weak to offer a true healing experience. The fantastic work of health care workers in saving lives and easing pain is appreciated daily, but it simply does us no good until we're in imminent danger. Emergent and urgent medical care is not our primary responsibility—that's why we call it *tertiary* care.

Society's increasing litigiousness is an interesting example of misdirected responsibility. Doctors and drug companies live in the same blame-game world as their patients. Because doctors exclusively credit the medicine when things go well, patients are obliged to blame the same for any disasters—and a vicious cycle is assured, if not insured.

Bureaucratic neurosis and red tape contribute to illness as much as our personal adhesions. Insurance snafus and coverage conundrums create a good share of needless anxiety and certain death. Remember that a healthy percentage of death and disability is caused by casual treatment, medication error, and ineligible scribble. Still, these medical horrors pale in comparison with the over-medicated and undereducated masses just spinning their wheels, awaiting their turn.

Responsibility at the Level of the Mind

> *Life is not something to be fixed,*
> *but something to be understood.*
> — Rachel Naomi Remen

Curator means "*to care for*" and profound curing requires somewhat of a caretaker as well as caregiver to look after the mind, body, and soul. No *one* cure works for everyone. *All* cures work for someone. Something about the person must make the final ruling. But the patient is at a loss to allow healing from the same stance where symptoms began. Healing begins in earnest with the repair of perceptions about health and illness.

Teachers, doctors, and the clergy together with social and political leaders are in powerful positions to change people's lives. Their loving or commanding presence can create the healing radiance that resonates with the essential wholeness of each person in their flock. Yet, only a highly integrated vision can perceive the extreme depth of that opportunity and responsibility.

The world's obvious evil that gets our attention is relatively rare and easier to deal with, if not after the fact. The shocking abuse of children by teachers, clergy, and parents is made infinitely worse by the betrayal of their oaths and the abuse of their authority. Morally beneath the law, these "*people of the lie*" respectfully posture themselves in positions behind the law.

Only our lack of appreciation of the lifetime harm inflicted on youngsters could keep the rest of society from treating these people as true psychological slayers. These sins-of-the-fathers show a denial so strong we can't even imagine where it came from—unless we examine our own.

Somehow, we're less interested in subtle nastiness perpetrated daily by our friendly neighborhood professionals. The strict and biased views of social institutions, schools, and places of worship inadvertently cultivate a lot of the social stigma, shame, and prejudice against particular affections and afflictions. And although a person's power to overcome is enormous, that power is rapidly defused by the respected elders who think they know better.

Uneducated people of lower socio-economic means fill up the majority of hospitals and prisons. But it's not merely because they're uneducated and poor. Their lifestyle and living conditions are undeniably shaped by their inner world. Possibilities, power, and hope shrink to nothing when developmental identity in purpose, love, and responsibility is diminished.

Similarly, the average lottery winner promptly returns to his pre-winning lifestyle and personality, if not friends. Yet, the high school drop-out-cum-millionaire is undeterred by inevitable bankruptcies to bring home the bacon—and the point. Money that lasts, like inner wealth, simply reflects a valued identity and self-worth. While both examples are surely products of their upbringing and experience, each is also a *work-in-progress* with the innate means to respond to life.

We can glimpse how responsible we are by the dramatics of our responses to the daily barrage of bad news. No one can completely escape the culture's sensationalized fascinations and revulsions. But our own indignation, outrage, blame, and vengeance are very revealing. Our reactive weapon of choice is exposed by how offended, defensive, or contentious we become—our inclination to fight, flee or cringe.

True, we feel insulted, humiliated, or diminished in some way. Then, of course it's natural to lash out, protect ourselves, or belittle someone else. But in reality, the personal attack cuts so deeply simply because our identity is so superficial. Our tantrum is really a mini identity crisis acting out in plain view to remind us of our *dis*-integrated persona. We can all take some credit for adding to the rage that spills all over the evening news.

If this inner fistfight snowballs enough, we might be scapegoating foreign citizens and screaming to sacrifice more criminals while hailing tighter borders and stronger penalties. Eventually we're holding placards and cheering at the hangings. Now we *are* the evening news.

Thankfully, cultural sacrifices have evolved over the centuries, as we were willing to give up less and less of our physical selves in return for a divine blessing. From the offering up of a whole virgin to just a finger, then, from an animal to a fiery symbol, someone or something would pay for our favor in denial of our own responsibility.

Now, at a time when we know sacrifice to really mean giving up our comfy but confused identity for a more righteous one, with the promise of health and happiness—screw it. It's easier to hang some other bastard. The collateral damage of society's meaningless punishments allows the innocent masses to remain in denial, inadvertently creating the atmosphere for the criminal extremes. All the while, the misunderstood villain plots his revenge on the unsuspecting and unexamined society. The message from kindergarten rings loud and clear—don't get caught.

Our schooling in punitive damage left most of us with the notion that public punishment serves as an example that deters unruly behavior—of course, the bad seeds never did pay much attention in class. Nothing sends them a message faster or stronger than society's unspoken messages of exemplary errors. Inadvertently sent and subliminally received, the hypnotic suggestion of our combined character cultivates much of the criminal intent.

Responsibility at the Level of the Soul

> *It's easier to fight for one's principles,*
> *than to live up to them.*
> — Alfred Adler

When we finally find it in our hearts to claim some tiny responsibility for the most horrific crimes against humanity, we'll feel in our souls the right to consider a miniscule kinship with the most righteous among us.

It was only *there but for the grace of God* that we were able to side-step becoming one of the dregs of society. But while our heads were down, we missed the heroic feats and inexplicable generosity of a few rare souls. The impoverished scholars and entrepreneurs, disabled athletes and courageous veterans, against all odds and with few resources, brilliantly display the triumphant of the human spirit that we all could embody.

The enlightened spirit still needs the lowly mind to reveal its brilliance. A multi-hued, ageless, and trans-gender soul fizzles in the darkened corner of a disintegrated world view. Through the tainted glass of a lost soul the world indeed appears darkly as *us versus them*.

Racism, sexism, age-ism, and the rest reflect the schism in those identities—the cracked mirror of a schizoid personality. Where else could such an unnatural distaste of natural phenomena originate but from an abnormal and tasteless self-image? The same mechanism occurs in love as it's impossible to embrace those aspects of a wife that a husband has rejected in himself—like the feminine aspects—and vice versa. All this rage-ism represents a fight for distinction in a world cut off from our ultimate sameness. These radical responses show how a droplet of ignorance obscures a whole sea of souls.

By suppressing frightening ideas, we communally trip the fault line for overblown tremors. Then, the extremist views find eventual release in extreme behavior. Over-the-hedge ecologists, ridiculous feminists, and animalistic activists, like right-for-lifers and begging choosers, all have a point. But the purpose gets lost amongst their exaggerated, disturbing, and often violent demonstrations.

Fanatics and idealists with tiny truths become caricatures of their mangled personalities. Parading gays, fundamentalist faiths, and supremacist militias aren't seriously considered because of their inflammatory and cartoonish rhetoric. But a responsible understanding of where they all come from and how they all got here holds meaning for our own spiritual healing.

If we prepare for the worst we might expect the best. Suffering leisurely in the comfort of our own home, we can learn vicariously through sorrowful others around the corner and around the world. With enough empathy or interest, we can almost imagine and certainly examine the plight of the homeless, the hungry, and the devastated. We might just be inclined to do something about it.

It's not the same as actually living through the trauma, but it's a better thought experiment than turning away in horror, crossing our fingers, and hoping it never happens to us. This play-acting served us well enough during childhood as our most productive learning tool. When life comes calling, and it will, there's precious little time to ponder the meaning of life-threatening situations.

If the best we can do is pity the fool and be glad it's not us, then we'll have little to offer when it's someone we care about. On the other hand, our fearless forethought adds to the afterglow of our loving presence. We can literally hold the healing torch that lights the way for others, if only because we've taken our responsibility seriously.

Aging and Death

> *You can't have a peaceful life*
> *without a peaceful understanding about death,*
> *and you won't have a peaceful death*
> *without a peaceful understanding about life.*
> — Dali Lama

The monopoly of medicine, like the dominance of technology, is due to its obvious impact—the big saves. Housing, sanitation, and immunization, like pre-natal care, get us over the hump, and emergency surgery saves it.

But the real reasons for happiness and longevity are plainly seen through the smiling spirits of our longest lived. Inevitably, we'll find a shining optimism, strength to cope with losses, a golden purpose, and independence for living and thinking. That sounds like love, responsibility, purpose, and freedom. These old souls haven't even had much contact with doctors and hospitals, while their lifestyles are all over the board.

It's no wonder our potential lifespan is as unused as our grey matter. Biologists get so excited about extending life with genetic technology, but we can't even use the hundred and something year span we already have. It ain't broke.

Even if and when the medicos could guarantee us our century of disease free years, it would be maddening without the antidote for cynicism, boredom, pettiness, and the unrelenting fear of death! Suicides would skyrocket—not to mention law suits, divorces, and insurance rates. If all disease was cured today, we'd all be forced to learn about responsible healing at the level of the soul.

Aging doesn't automatically mean disease. Neglected imbalances create the inflamed indulgences that aggravate the normal degenerative changes. Then, a myriad of microbes, behaviors, and toxins add fuel to the fire that begins a slow burn. Only a twisted fear would try to blame it all on the time. Health and disease are ongoing processes rather than static end products. But we can't see that until we fire up our own healing hearth.

Excessive age-related disability and deterioration are a combination of given circumstances plus our own added dimensions. The stress within the embattled psyche is enough to leave its scars on the body throughout the ages. Like most daily disorders, dysfunction with aging is largely gratuitous. Hardly anybody dies of old age these days.

Just as a soulful love can sustain the sex and romance in whatever customized fashion, the deepest responsibility can preserve much of the vim and vigor of weary organs. There's a lot of biological redundancy built into even the most dilapidated kidneys. Like the brain, we're most certainly not using any organ to its fullest capacity.

Growing older in its true context is not to be confused with the rampant denial of aging and death. Invoking love and purpose to ease pain and anxiety while increasing function, is not the same as feigning youth with cosmetic cures, sporty cars, and disposable companions. Speaking of the grace of an aging body tells a different tale than the awkwardness of masking the truth.

How old we get as we age is our responsibility. Depending on our perceptual enrollment, we can select the standard or accelerated programs in physiology and psychology. Notice how fearless, fun lovers seem to hang around forever. And they're the ones that are happy to go at any time. Orchestra conductors and comedians have the greatest longevity. Music and humor—go figure.

The importance of responsibility is realized in all our pain and suffering when taken as opportunities to grow. As our identity transcends body and mind, fears of morbidity and mortality fade in a shining *joi de vivre*. When we loosen the grip on life, we can breathe easy.

Death, being our biggest crisis (hopefully) endows life with its most meaning. As we identify with the meaning in our life, we fear less because we love more. Our immortality is assured in the meaning of everything and everyone we touch. Saving time, money, and energy from preventing the inevitable affords us the time to invest in an extraordinary life right now, while it lasts.

So we do end up doing something, but it's subtle. We take responsibility, but we take it easy. We do less, but we accomplish more. We don't live for the weekends, holidays, and retirement. We don't milk the system for everything we think we're worth, work to rule, or point fingers. We don't deny all pain and hardship at the risk of making things worse. We make fewer mistakes, learn faster, and cope better. That's something.

Comfort at the controls of this powerful dynamic eases the mind with the sweet assurance that the body will take care of itself. With the help of a relaxed metabolic response, repair and renewal are enlivened along with immunity, digestion, elimination, and sleep. The lack of responsibility is a profound risk factor for chronic, degenerative disease that hides beneath the highly touted cholesterol, blood pressure, and percentage body fat.

The truth and meaning of responsibility are known directly in the sincere and respectful way we confront life's highs and lows. By fulfilling purpose and love, responsibility generates an absolute power that appeases the appetite to abuse any provisional power. Taking our assigned seat in the universe gives us the poise and the style that only comes from doing the driving.

The seams holding the organizing, joining, and resistive tendencies together in life are somewhat decorative. The fundamental strands of purpose, love, and responsibility are interwoven into an evolving and spiraling dynamic that literally becomes our conscious awareness. Our way in the world is already set by *why, how,* and *what* we do. Yet, with a promising new caring and commanding character, we just upped the ante for life's most enduring pleasure—the joy of a bona fide freedom.

* * *

Interpreting Freedom

Health is not particularly funny. But neurosis, now that's funny. Love is not very funny. But mother-in-laws are a laugh riot. Problems and stupidity get big laughs because we can all relate. The best comedians have parlayed their angst into fame and fortune. The great ones never let the civility of success take the "hood" out of the hoodlum. I didn't want to become so happy and healthy that I completely lost my sense of humor. The often-giggling spiritual masters suggest to me that mean-spirited and toilet humor can evolve into the intelligent entendres, double takes, and catch-22s of a truly divine comedy. Who's on first?

I modestly assumed I had an eye for aesthetics or a taste for the finer things. The colors and qualities of my clothes, artwork, and furnishings easily mixed and matched over the years and the relocations. Even my girlfriends seemed a perfect fit as they shared a substance and authentic beauty that was truly fine. I only cared for enduring things and I happily went without if my choices were out of reach, which they usually were. In time, I came to realize the common thread in all my cotton, oak, brass, glass, stone, plants, and fine art—they were all real. And so were the girlfriends. ☺

I often pleaded, "Stop the world, I want to get off." Yet, vacations never did much for me. I've been miserable in some of the most beautiful places in the world. The problem was that I went with me. I needed a vacation from myself. Drugs were too scary and I would still be ugly in the morning. There's no point in paying to get away until I enjoy my own company. Geography alone is not going to do it. I decided not to go away anymore just to get away, but only to travel with something greater in mind. In the meantime, "Bartender, another cubra libre please."

My best friends seemed to make their own breaks, go with the flow, and walk on the sunny side of life. I'll never forget how forgiving they've been to my relatively broken promise, windless sails, and cloudy disposition. It was painfully clear to me that there is a way in the world with less hang-ups, hold-ups, and letdowns that had nothing to do with the world itself. I knew I would know it when I see it.

Rumors of my impending marriage were enough for me to be suddenly and dramatically included, invited, and respected as a successful member of society. I think I was the same person the day before. Anyway, after the divorce, I was surprised to learn how much I indeed worried what other people thought of me. I had exaggerated the honest need for acceptance and the understandable need to be understood. But a huge burden lifts when you know for certain a whole big bunch of people already think you're a moron—there's nothing to worry about. So that was good.

I thought that any type of society could work if everyone grew up and behaved. Philosopher kings or benevolent dictators would be great if they actually existed. In my dreams, a powerful group of soulful thinkers with altruistic ideals, free of ambition, greed, and ulterior motives would advise the lesser powers that be. As much as I am proud of being Canadian, only someone in a free and decent society has the luxury and the responsibility to critically examine the good, bad, and ugly with an eye toward a greater meaning of freedom.

The Meaning of Freedom

You can't force people to be free.
— Ken Wilber

If we were truly free we would be more honest with ourselves. We would do what we know is right, strive for what we love, and mean what we say. We would be free of the physical, emotional, and social pressures that divert time and attention from our best interests. The type of freedom that releases us from the chains of social and emotional conditioning is an inside job.

Political freedom is a secondary expression, the social product of the subjective liberties and rights that are already achieved by the majority of citizens. The democratic social order, then, in turn creates the public milieu conducive to further evolution of personal freedom, more so than any written edict. Importantly, the relief of collective oppression does indeed allow a psychic independence that contributes more to our increasing longevity than all the medical technology, lifestyle choices, or genetic mutations. Still, the legalities don't guarantee that our version of happiness will bear fruit.

Simple awareness of our legislated freedoms does inspire a more cheerful will to live. But the legal rights that can be seized when we're suspected of a crime are different than the soulful self-rule that saves our hides when we're wrongly convicted.

The painstaking history of civilization is the excruciatingly slow, but sure, evolution of personal autonomy. In fact, it's this self-sufficiency that inspires people to rally for universal equality and opportunity. Still, the leading edge of freedom fighters forever drags a pigheaded craze of cowboys, pining for the good old days of slave labor, barefoot wives, and the supremacy of white guys.

Legal freedom obliges lawful duties. Democratic rights demand social responsibilities. But heartily seizing our full sovereign opportunity requires the power of personal responsibility. Only the sizeable but tender strength of love and will can lasso any fears of our newfound freedom.

Look, it's a lot easier to follow the leader, buy into an idea, and not rock the boat. It's scarier and more demanding to trust our own leadership, aspire to new ventures, and chart our own course. For lack of confidence, courage, and conviction, it's simpler to sacrifice the vast unknown in lieu of more certain waters and to give up some freedom for well known, if well worn, restraints.

But if the foreboding waters die down, the headstrong winds of responsibility can fill our sails enough to leave the shallow shores. True love, then, releases our creaky and weary emotional backstays, while genuine purpose lets out some line on that resistant and rusty intellectual boom. Innate courage can then unfurl like a spinnaker from the heart so that the soul can hike out to its rightful place amongst a regatta of independent thinkers, dreamers, and lovers to discover the true meaning of freedom.

The Nature of Freedom

> *Happiness can't be pursued,*
> *it must ensue.*
> — Viktor Frankl

Like unconditional relationships, we were born with inalienable rights. No matter the incivility of our particular society, we maintain our right to know ourselves and be ourselves. But just as our innate duty is to purpose and love, this *free reign* is our responsibility. Just how well we finesse our freedom depends on careful planning.

Authentic freedom is clearly absent in the widespread neuroses, addiction, and crime in our streets. Immediate gratification, ulterior motives, and hidden agendas reveal the easy enticements to a weakened mind and a weary body. Media, parental, and peer pressure progressively can wear down even the toughest resolve. Any lasting freedom from our own compulsive cravings, contorted concepts, and subconscious conflicts is beyond the reach of pop psychology, popping pills, and surgical steel. No, the final frontier of freedom is up to us.

Responsibility and love are about connections and associations. Purpose and freedom are about being unique and distinct. These apparent opposites can only be reconciled from a view of the highest value. A similar catch-22 is seen in all body-mind quandaries, male-female questions, and science-religion conundrums. The perceptual keys to this Pandora of paradox are in the pockets of a wider and clearer context.

Free will is only as free as the line of sight through which we see our choices. This perceptual insight determines the degree of self-determination that we can fly in the pre-determined face of destiny, genes, or God. It makes sense that human reality allows for contingency plans and accidents, chance and necessity, just like the rest of reality. Rather than a reckless disregard for others, the spontaneity of ultimate freedom forever aligns with universal integrity and values.

Free love is not really about wild, indiscriminate, and anonymous sex. Darn. Rather, loving freely means having relationships without being had by them and depending upon them without utter dependence. To love freely is to respect and support a loved one's sovereignty—no strings attached.

Because intellectual and emotional freedom offers more information, choices, and maybe some wisdom, the odds of stumbling across a soul mate, a soul purpose, or a sole solution dramatically improve—and with them, a shot at a generous, creative, or constructive response.

If purpose means to "*use it or lose it*," freedom means to "*love it and leave it*" alone. It means caring without cramping, holding without strangling, and letting go without dropping. While purpose encourages us with "*try it, you'll like it,*" freedom inspires us to use "*everything in moderation, except moderation.*"

By moderating the extremes of attraction and repulsion, acceptance and rejection, we're free of our own personal extremism. Freedom means enjoying everything more, but needing everything less. It means having it all without the need to own it all. They can't take that away.

As responsibility offers a subtle honest power, freedom promises a certain lasting joy. Each increment in freedom opens ecstatic new worlds, golden moments, and simple pleasures. Even one solemn moment in the throws of absolute freedom awakens us like nothing we can imagine or anything anyone else could offer.

Enduring happiness assuredly appears in the clearing as a peaceful contentment when the clinging fog of excessive needs are negotiated, balanced, and lifted. Our hunger for quantity is now appeased with a taste for quality. An indulgence is only a vice if it has a firm grip on us. That bottomless cup, habitual highball, or grinning sweet tooth is slowly refined as we're reformed into a connoisseur of coffee, cognac, or chocolate. When a gifted gourmet steps in for the glutton, we can hand in our fake ID and concede who we really are—a cappella.

The Freedom of Nature

> *Life is what happens
> while we're making other plans.*
> — John Lennon

The finest level of freedom is really fun. Infinite potential and immeasurable possibility rides the quantum information waves, growing and changing with trial and error. Primordial learning is limitless and fancy free as creativity plays itself out. Formalities follow function *ad infinitum* as particles endlessly change their stripes, weaving in and out between the one and the many.

The laws of nature follow form in downhill thermodynamics. Taking the path of least resistance, chaotic entropy randomly ensues. This wilding still finds time and energy to dovetail with the self-ordering, cooperative, and responsive color schemes to re-aim, re-fashion, and re-create some semblance of order. In this way, the *neg*-entropic surge of creative evolutionary design busts through.

This evolving force of natural law slips through the rather limiting physical and biological laws with an explosive array of species, shapes, and sizes. This hardly seems necessary to sustain the long flourishing and stoic mass of microbes and mosquitoes. But even if completely by chance, the growing diversity of flora and fauna increases the odds for continued variety.

Finite genetic machinations give birth to infinite biological permutations and combinations. The spontaneous novelty, innovation, and ingenuity of genetic mutation paint an irrefutable picture of biofreedom, no matter how deaf, dumb, or blind. The resulting life forms are then selectively massaged by environmental responses for universal benefit, no matter how haphazard, mistaken, or injurious.

Biology describes, but cannot explain, just exactly how and why all the liveliness succeeds against a life-defying riptide of decay, deterioration, and disorder. But it's no illusion that *life* was born in the stars and that *mind* eventually crawled out from under the rocks. The spiritual heights of human freedom are forever enslaved and indebted to these earthly and heavenly origins—for all practical purposes.

It's hard not to *Disney-fy* all the meandering molecular happenstance in the original animated feature. Language itself is a dizzying projection of our need for self-expressive certainty. Plus, the elemental lingo and genetic jargon that play supporting roles in all material life are the understudies for our human word pictures.

Alternatively, the details of science are always in flux, usually negotiable, and likely way off. Even if we deem this metaphor to be meaningless and the centuries of mystic wisdom a charming coincidence, it just doesn't matter. Our health and the meaning of health have not come undone.

The essential energy of purpose, love, responsibility, and freedom forever fill the void in our wide open soul. It still satisfies needs, prevents needless suffering, and assures the strength to cope and overcome. Oh yeah, not to forget. These heady independents also direct and executive-produce the original scores for better diagnosis, treatment, and technology.

	Purpose	**Love**	**Responsibility**	**Freedom**
Quantum	order	correlated	interactive	potential
Atomic	design	attraction	resistive	entropy
Biological	instinct	symbiosis	selection	mutation
Emotional	desire	nurture	commitment	dreams
Intellectual	goals	marriage	laws	democracy
Soulful	spontaneity	presence	responsive	carefree

Freedom at the Level of Things

> *What lies behind us and what lies before us are tiny matters compared to what lies within us.*
> — Ralph Waldo Emerson

There's nothing bad about our possessions, unless they possess us. There's nothing bad about our money, until it owns us. Even physical sensation itself is as good as it gets, when given its proper respect. We could delight in tasting everything beautiful, if need and greed didn't inflame the ugly hunger for more and more.

Purpose indulges the senses, while the pride of freedom is in not over indulging. Sensual balancing is perpetually necessary to quell the urgency of the lower needs. Puzzling habits and addictions aren't reducible to genotype or phenotype. It gets embarrassing by the time we're searching for the shopping gene. Inclinations and leanings of any body type can be inflamed just as the obsession with any talent. Genetic tendencies are layered in a person's psychological perspective, then wrapped in extensive social and cultural conditioning.

Therefore, the alcoholic and the chocoholic alike have the psychology to indulge and the biology to overindulge long before they ever imbibe and long after they're dry. But forever chaining them to the diagnostic label is itself an addiction that enslaves their identity to something they *have*, not something they *are*. By blaming the genes and judging the personality, we shirk our responsibility, forget our love, bind our purpose, and confine our freedom. People are simply more than the current state of their dispositions and affinities.

But they're not alone. The body suffers its own mistaken identity, forgets its purpose, and bilks its responsibility to become an even worse enemy. We're not born with sensitivities, allergies, and inflammatory illnesses—we just swung that way. Like addictions, most allergies and inflammatory conditions begin more functional than physical, more physiological fiction than fact. Eventually, though, our worst fears are realized through distorted assumptions, aggravating consumptions, and then, sadly, our need to be believed.

Autoimmune disorders like rheumatoid arthritis that attack linings and coverings of organs and joints are dynamic imbalances rather than static diseases of single gene errors. Consider the years of conditioning by mysterious stimuli, multiple toxins, and mindless habits mixed up with cultural taboos, genetic tendencies, and mechanistic treatment all perceived by an innocent patient who is told the whole experience is absolutely meaningless. NEXT.

When we attend to our physical, mental, and spiritual needs, then innate biological responsiveness can be remembered, rejuvenated, or at least a little more reasonable. Caring for the continuum of needs encourages normal healing mechanisms to naturally drift back toward business as usual.

We don't even need to cure everything, nor can we. We just need to care enough to recall to that sub-clinical balance—before *things got worse*. That's the undervalued care that gets lost in the midst of fixations with quick medicinal cures. Innate healing is the only mechanism that cures anything that can be cured. What can't be cured, though, can be better tolerated, tempered, or outright transcended. Like love and will, freedom from the body is seriously subjective.

Free enterprise is free to capitalize on our fear of freedom. Unknowingly but willingly, we surrender our freedom, broken under the persuasive media pressure. Advertising tempts us by mixing and matching our wholesome needs with wholesale goods. This mutual conspiracy against the truth in advertising cons us into all the desired labels and designer logos. Our choices for what is in our best interests are taken up by cheap give-a-ways and expensive lay-a-ways. We opt for no money down, unconsciously committing future earnings to past yearnings.

Think about the percentage of the economy that is supported by businesses whose best interests are their own, adding little or nothing to society's needs. At best, these companies add to the creativity of the owners, the paychecks of the employees, sometimes with a bit of fun and popular craziness. But all the charity work in the world by the fat conglomerate cats can't make up for the cultural inertia induced by glutting the marketplace. Then, the real biggies *go global*, targeting untapped island markets, thereby wiping out any hope of personal freedom for the poor and hungry kids around the world who worship western excess.

But they give us what we want and we couldn't afford to get rid of them, even we wanted to. It's a vicious currency cycle founded on titillating needs and teasing imbalances. They've got us by the short and curlies and we've sold our soul for the lowest offer.

Business values can change, however slowly, along with the sluggish values of society. If and when the CEO grows up, he either changes the company's mission statement or he parts company on principle. Only an irrational purpose or desperate fear could explain how educated people can sell harmful or useless products with a seemingly clear conscience. Only a profound ignorance of their own spiritual enslavement could allow them to sell their soul to the highest bidder. So we're kind of *even, Steven.*

The meaning of desires, cravings, and entertainment excesses becomes clear in the light of knowing that most businesses would file for bankruptcy without them—including health care. For the majority of gratuitous businesses, it's the meaning of harm that is drastically reduced or completely discounted.

In the meantime, our wallets are bulging with 2-for-1 coupons, discount passes, and get-one-free cards. Everyone's a VIP and the gold on our card means we graduated from high school. We chase points, miles, and stamps like gerbils on wheels to win prizes we don't need or things we don't want. If we're checking the coupon book to know what we feel like for dinner, maybe they've....*Gotcha*. Whim shopping has crept into whim medicine—*would you like a pap smear with that, Ma'am?*

When "*The Good Life*" promised at the local hospital is the name of their fundraiser lottery—not to worry. The government-sponsored casinos and lottos will fund any gambling addictions. The true values of health are a long shot from the actual values of the health care business. The unspoken and unspeakable message to the kids and the community rings louder than all the coins raised for research—something for nothing.

Real freedom comes as we lessen the hold on our sensitive jewels. We'll appreciate the sensation more without all the sensationalism. We'll take more pleasure in tasting everything, but we'll take less. It's the quality of our relationship with all our stuff that determines its value to our greater goodness. How conscientious a consumer or barbaric a buyer we become relates to how and why we shop in the first place and the meaning of all that stuff.

As priorities change, a lot of our junk becomes a burden and a distraction and we'll feel like liquidating some assets. The garage seems full of things not worth insuring, securing, and worrying about anymore. We can exchange all our excessive belongings to receive the spiritual credit—free of charge. The freedom to walk away from time-limited offers comes when items with purpose, love, or responsibility take up most of our discretionary spending. By the time we chuckle when something is lost, stolen, or broken, we'll know that a sense of spiritual humor took root where material insecurity once grew.

Freedom at the Level of Thoughts

> *The only real freedom*
> *is freedom of thought.*
> — Ken Wilber

    Rigid reasoning, flighty feelings, and inactive imagination are the synaptic ties that bind. Just as balancing the senses relieves physical cravings, honoring the full mental spectrum is the path to a free and open mind. Satisfying our subjective needs fulfills the deficits in our attention and the defaults in our personality. A little mind control is better than a lot of mindless occupations.

    Most anxiety and angst is heightened by limited options, minimal resources, with few prospects on the horizon. Impulsive reactions, irrational choices, and poor coping strategies are born again in a tiny perceptual world. The mounting stress has us clinging to old comforts, seeking quick and simple solutions. By the time we've indeed sculpted the so-called *chemical imbalance,* our scattered brain accurately reflects our wandering mind. Now anybody would be happy for a little doctoring—just to top things up.

    When teased and tormented, everyday likes and dislikes gel into cloying attachments and shocking aversions. When enraged, they morph into neurotic obsessions and deadly repulsions. Over time, this inner turmoil hardens into the scary phobias and philias of long neglected signs. This world of scarcity is graduate studies for greed and intolerance. Facing life honestly is frightening enough, but it's petrifying with this mental anarchy. And we thought we were free.

    Evil behavior is often assumed to be the result of free will when in fact the ill will is anything but free. In order to distance ourselves from the worst of humanity, we need to deny that their distorted perceptions, insecure identities, and disordered personalities could be just a matter of degree. But any will is only as free as its balance in purpose and love. And its interests are only as good as its perception of possible responses. Reckless, selfish, and harmful behavior is the result of an identity enslaved to the inclinations, imbalances, and conditioning that sees no other way out—the same as everyday sin.

A personality disorder is simply a disordered purpose that is lacking a little personality. By enjoying a range of intellectual exercises and imaginative gymnastics, the mind maintains a more accepting, more patient, and less mangled existence. Engaging in an immensity of ideas and a diversity of disciplines allows the development of all faculties including intuition, insight, and inventiveness.

With authentic *freedom of information,* one tends to unload needless intellectual property. The lines are now free for incoming calls. We're free to utilize the wealth of information in the annals of academia in the greatest context with greater authority for all it's worth. Our best choices now ensure that we have no fault trials and guilt-free errors. Free of duress from outside pressure or expectation, our inner referencing system allows us a unique response. We *can* have it all without it having us.

With the balanced refinement of our full character, even bizarre interests, inane inclinations, and outlandish ideologies are not without tongue firmly in cheek. Combined with some study, logic, and common sense, we might pay more attention, ask bigger questions, and develop a taste for meaning. With this experience, we're free to lighten our relationships and power our responses to any mishaps and missteps we happen to step in. Our mere presence now brings both sides to the table.

Experiencing, knowing, and identifying with all thoughtful things allows us to relate to a variety of views. All cultures, clubs, and communities ring true. The sense of belonging to the human race, global life, and the universe relieves us from any unreasonable longing for spousal, societal, and cultural partnership. This intellectual independence allows a genuine *freedom of association* that is on our own terms of our own accord.

Discrimination is a warning sign that incriminates the margins of our identity. Covert suppression of our personality becomes the overt oppressor of others. Freely rejoicing in the celebrations, pageantry, and food of other cultures comes by experiencing the common bonds of human circumstance behind all the pomp.

Actual *freedom of religion* can't happen before freedom *from* religion. The cultured eye pierces the differences among congregations, covenants, and cultures. Careful insights and greater perspectives of all traditions release any self-righteousness. Each hallowed healing path leads to the same universal truths by reminding us of our own sacred nature. When we see it in our heart to visit any temple and partake in any practice, we'll understand the meaning of religion. Without mistaking the rhetoric for the reality, we'll know that our faith is a freely chosen one.

We're born free, but it's a poorly informed freedom. True freedom is an enlightened freedom. As our identity soars over demographics, genealogy, and prep schools, we'll earn a degree of freedom that brings enduring reasons to pass the ball onto the next generation. The whole family experience is enjoyed more when it's free of parental pressure and cultural baggage.

Each person will resonate more with some ideologies than with others. However, now they are absent of the resentment, disrespect, and contempt for other people's choices. It's funny that free choice was there all along but, let's just say, somewhat indisposed. Self-determination boldly steps up to the plate as we find our own rhythm, make our own breaks, and go with the flow of life's mysterious currents. Once all the fussing and fidgeting is finished, worlds of possibilities open up for us to truly seize the day—*Carpe Diem*.

When the band stops playing and the tunes finally fade, the mind awakens in an endless field where the lyrics are first written and melodies are first heard. When the cocooned identity becomes one and the same as the mother of invention, a free spirit flies away.

The Free Spirit

I have no plans, I have no hope, I am free.
— Buddhist Aphorism

A free spirit is something like happy-go-lucky or devil-may-care. But being carefree is far from careless. These beautiful souls are concerned but not consumed, involved but not interned. Not so bothered by bothersome things, the free spirit enjoys the sensuality without being seduced and the sentiment without being set up. Since intrigue, beauty, and meaning can always be found, the free spirit releases any undue regret or anticipation.

If purpose, love, and responsibility are *why, how,* and *what* we do, then freedom is considerate of *when* we finally get around to it. And freedom is now. For the ultimate freedom beyond space and matter, the only thing left is the time. Somewhere between past and future, cause and effect, there exists a place before time—the timeless miracle of our present awareness.

The value of time must be true because it keeps reoccurring. Physics, psychology, and mysticism all chime in when it comes to the time. In quantum physics, the charts and graphs have no timeline because at the finest level of material reality, time is relatively meaningless. Backwards and forwards are equally topsy turvy as everything somehow happens at once.

Analytical psychology says that we're stuck in the past. People, places, and possessions are prejudged through miserable memories of bygone eras. Even plans for the future are prejudicial in light of this jet-lagged awareness. These symptoms are suggestive that some early trauma is a stumbling block to our prospective development. The therapist will say that *living in the past* is only resolved by probing the retained matter in attempts to release the blockage.

Mystic poets speak of an eternal and timeless awareness that can only be held in our present moment experience with the release of all ties to the past and the future. They encourage us to allow this blissful feeling to seep into our workaday lives. But who's got that kind of time?

Observing life's seasonal rhythms, the ancient cultures calibrated them, named them, and followed them. Now we've become enslaved to the days of the week, months of the year, and the zodiac signs. Interestingly, leap years, date-lines, and time zones all serve to remind us that we can toy with time by turning it back and springing it forward. We can toast New Year's Eve twice in a row while cruising across the International Date Line—*as if you're not already ordering doubles.*

Cultural time is a mental construction to clock the speed of passing perceptions—an *illusion of the senses,* if you will. This mechanical nature of time helps us keep track of things so we're not late for work. And although the actual arrow of time dissipates in one direction of three-dimensional space, we just made it up. But it's the kind of measure that tends to blur the meaning of time with respect to biology.

We have time on our hands while we watch it slip through our fingers. We're always pressed for it, there's never enough of it, and we're always trying to beat it. We stretch it out, fill it in, and put it in, but inevitably, time runs out. The common pressuring, bulging, and bleeding diseases are the final gasps of a stressful, hurried life.

Of course, our sense of time is the inevitable result of our relationship with all our sensations. As we surrender our identity with thoughts and things, we begin to truly enjoy ourselves and have a better time. Once we release our death grip on the passing fun, we might just gain a timeless sense of joy.

The purity of present is a sacred gift that is not really given. This greatest gift is actually captured by the quality of attention of a loving presence. Similarly, a healing radiance operates not as some secret transmission, but as a suspended moment of utter trust and acceptance. Clear of regret or worry, we can still plan and remember, but for the moment, we're free.

The immediate present is the original inspired moment. *In spirit*, the mind is free to honor the honest ideas that keep popping up. This is the ever-present wellspring of creativity, imagination, and dreams. It's the source of endless possibilities, potentials, and promises for our best intentions, vital interests, and honored guesses.

The full strength of character gains its poise from the identification with this defining moment. The clearest attention and most passionate intention live here, welcoming the most powerful and creative impulses. Their subsequent presence exhibits quite a commanding performance. There's no need to bring personalities into this because freedom tends to drop the attitude, along with the IQ, gender, and race.

Somehow, the secret of life, the fountain of youth, and the meaning of health all find sanctuary in the moment between before and after. How agile we remain while we age represents our rapport with space, matter, and time. Although the years and the mirrors don't lie outright, the wisdom and grace of a life well lived are closer than they appear when we're slightly ahead of our time.

A religious sensibility arises from this spiritual sensitivity that transcends domineering dogma and New Age flakiness. Any membership, following, or joining is now purely out of love rather than fear, grace rather than guilt, and social pleasure instead of pressure. Not to worry, we'll still appear normal to the mere mortals among us.

Freedom satisfies a subtle risk factor for illness that hides in the shadow of the morbidly obese ones. Freedom's magic comes in the immeasurable dimensions of our free-wheeling lifestyle. Free of a clingy body and a cloying mind, a noticeable ease disseminates throughout our physiology, our relationships, and our home. Released from conflicting values and contradictory advice, we can rest easy in our circadic healing and renewal rhythms. Even free thinking docs search for the best times to sleep, eat, medicate, and fornicate by studying the science of *chrono*-biology.

Purpose, love, responsibility, and freedom are finally free to harmonize together on a world tour. Each plays itself out through the billions of wonderfully strange and diverse human characters. But each also stands in as stunt double for the other. As lettered words, purpose, love, responsibility and freedom are weakly water colored. But as experiences, they hold a meaningful palate of all human highlights. Whether we like intention, attention, power, and pleasure or prefer meaning, optimism, coping, and independence—it just doesn't matter. We can clean our own slates and choose our own brushes—the meaning is the same: the meaning of health.

* * *

Intuitions of Mind

Being an artist trapped in a linebacker's body, eventually I felt resigned to study the sciences and complete the psychosis. And I wonder why no one understands me. I didn't know any streams other than mainstream, and first-year science was as comfy as repeating high school. I spent one morning looking into architecture and they sent me to environmental studies—whatever. Years later, confiding my missed calling to a patient, an architecture professor, I was assured that their curriculum leaves little to the imagination. What?

I had a completely scholarly interest in the bizarre extremes of psychic and spiritual phenomena, especially near-death experiences and spontaneous healing. They all were curious cultural phenomenon, but I was just as occupied with the testicular fortitude of the academics who discussed such things publicly. I enjoyed the debate, but there was no argument for me that something strange indeed was happening—however strangely interpreted. The frenzied reactions to unexplained phenomena taught me something about the imagined hysteria to everyday oohs and aahs.

Maybe the mind is ignored because it's too close to see without some high-powered mirror. The thinking process is so automatic as to be almost mundane. When I stop to think about it, the ability to think is more phenomenal than all the rare mental oddities and spirited peculiarities combined. Rocks evolved and began to think. What else do you need to know?

Science suggests that the mind is a secondary side effect of the brain that evolved through natural selection for survival advantage. But our brain hasn't mutated significantly in thousands of years. That means that all our psychological and cultural development has no survival value and is merely fantastic fun and of no real importance. No, the only way to squeeze the mind into a little object, like our brains, is with a massive cover up of personal insider information and shredding of secret subjective evidence.

The completed Human Genome Project is considered the greatest discovery since splitting the atom and landing on the moon. I'm still waiting for something more than the arms race and powdered orange juice. It sounds like artificial intelligence to manipulate genes to extend a life that isn't taken seriously. It reminds me of buying the best golf clubs in the world before you're breaking one hundred for eighteen holes. We're misusing our genes and brains to fix the genes and brains that are misusing our genes and brains—or something like that.

I was fascinated by twins and was caught staring on more than one occasion. Hey, I was doing important research. I know these identical twin doctors. One is a psychiatrist who likes his patients awake. The other one is an anesthetist who likes them asleep. One likes to talk to his patients, whereas the other one would rather not. They have identical genes, yet they have hugely different personalities. You would never mistake them, because their expressions, tone of voice, facial lines, postures, and personal manner clearly show that they're not identical at all. They taught me more about nature and nurture than any research study.

Meditation sounds great on paper. But something is missing in the translation. In any group of meditators, I never know if they just lost their personality or they never had one to begin with. What happened to the vitality, the vibrancy, and verve promised in the research and the brochure? I knew many people who seemed healthier and happier that would never even consider meditation. Still, I persevered for some reason.

It took me years before I stopped asking if I was doing this right or if that experience was wrong. The meditating masters inevitably have an answer for everything; they say everything is fine, but offer little explanation. I remember confiding in an Ayurvedic physician about finding my purpose in life. I actually paid money for him to say, "Just keep doing what you're doing." My brother could have told me that. But in fact, I think he said, "Why don't you stop doing what you're doing?"

The Meaning of Mind

It's beginning to sound as though health is all in our minds. Since purpose, love, responsibility, and freedom are vital aspects of health and essentially subjective, naturally the mind is a reasonable place to look. Now that we can see just how crucial the level of awareness is for well-being, closing our minds may indeed be a critical mistake. And agreeing that the best evidence is self-evident, we have some leeway with any scientific nitpicking.

Logic and reason constantly oscillate with intuition and imagination. The emotion and passion of mystic inspiration shares the logic and precision of scientific revelation. Old fashioned ignorance and steadfast denial are imperative if one ideological extreme is to flourish over the other. Just making the distinction between a male and a female thought requires a cultural stereotype or biological bias. By crossing the conceptual boundaries within our own minds, the pretense of personal, cultural, and geographical borders comes clear.

The mind was ex-communicated from the body about the time the church was separated from the state. It made sense to study separate realms separately, for practical and political purposes. Science kept to the mechanisms of natural phenomena while religion deciphered the meaning of supernatural phenomena. Of course, these distinctions are only as solid as the hypothetical walls that make it so. But the ancient fumes of this divisive conquering still linger among the modern remains.

The mind-body problem, as it were, rages on, cloaked in the various disguises of nature and nurture, liberal and conservative, male and female. In science, subjective flair still takes a back seat to objective estimates. But by stitching the tears in our ID tags, we can overcome this misleading squabble without being a backseat driver.

To the neurologist, the mind is an afterthought—the hallucinogenic fireworks display of brain cell chemistry. By admitting that physics can't explain life's animation, we realize the no-brainer that biology can't answer the call of the mind. The emerging mind, like the preceding life, is never content with its component parts. Cerebral structure and anatomical location will never fully explain the meaning of our corresponding experience.

It takes some enthusiastic mental gymnastics to use the mind to deny the mind. This arrogant agility is needed to secret our mind from the rest of our body. Once we identify with a sound body-brain, it's not a great leap to inadvertently deny our essential selves. But this psychological pyramid tumbles just as easily, when we broker a deal between the mind, the brain, and the body.

A bigger mystery than the body-mind brain-teaser is how everything blew into existence from nothing, how life dragged itself from a lifeless ocean, and how the mind woke up on a mindless planet. Those questions kind of put the kibosh on cleaning up the mind-body mess. Insights into the origin of our own ideas may be as close as we get to explain the creation of everything else.

A loftier vantage point, though, recognizes not two distinct realms but one continuous reality. Thoughts and things, like emotions and sensations, are all subjectively perceived as objects *in* conscious awareness. When we tone down the rhetoric, the conversation between the mind and the body is clear and concise—they speak the same language.

Oddly enough, it's time and time again that appears to resolve some of this *I and It* dislocation. Both our *psyche* and our *soma* contain information about past, present, and future. Mental and physical development can both be stunted and side tracked, but strange as it may sound, a lot of the information is somehow already there.

Each cell enfolds the chromosomal book of life—so it is written. Like immortal microbes, the genes hold the annals of our evolutionary past. Also, our possible physical futures are genetically programmed at the moment of conception. And warehouses of yet unexpressed DNA codes and combinations are the digital software of humanity's evolutionary future.

Similarly, fairy tales, dreams, and mythic archetypes of cultures past are mysteriously woven into our individual and collective subconscious.

The stages of psychological development emerge predictably and universally from birth. And considerate mystics across time and tradition share communal insights of our potent capacity for psychic growth.

Interestingly, both mental perceptions *and* physical sensations have the ability to get things moving. Emotions flood the body with cascading hormonal frenzies for the wildly moving experiences of anger, embarrassment, and sexual arousal. PET scan technology confirms indeed that *all* thoughts act like mini emotions, softly tickling the physiology and seducing the blood flow.

Of course, then the ravages of dreaming, sleeping, and waking consciousness would induce a steadier bodily imprint. It's doesn't take a big leap of faith to suggest that our unexamined traumas and repressed emotions are taking a long and silent toll on the body. More longstanding yet is the established development of our personal level of perception. From this identity platform, our current personality is the original gatekeeper and the lone interpreter of all waking experience and dreaming images, 'til death do us part.

That means that our very grounding in purpose, love, responsibility, and freedom kicks off the initial irresistible force—our mind, to the foremost immoveable object—our body. And then the fun really begins.

Multiple personality disorder is an extravagant example of how a change in identity dramatically impresses itself upon the physiology. Full blown diseases, allergies, addictions, metabolism, and even refractive error of the cornea have all been astonishingly altered to assume the fractured persona. This striking example of *physique imitating mystique* is left for dead in a mindless medicine. But it shows just what a colorful caricature we can make of ourselves with the right mental crayons.

We *can* fake it to make it, if we really mean it. Actors know how precise pretending can ignite very real emotions. Just watching a chick flick, goof ball comedy, or violent war epic will take us on a ride that diddles our immunity, our appetite, and our sleep. But we can't permanently trick the body into believing what we don't actually believe ourselves.

The sound of music is coded in palpable air waves that also create sensational motion. A human fetus makes precise muscular efforts to specific tunes. Babies and infants instinctively jive to the beat. If Grandpa's not too self-conscious, bored, or inebriated he might feel the ancient impulse to get up and hoof it. The devilish airwaves must have made him do it. We can still blame his sentimental mood if we like, which is fine.

The music is so *in us* that it's not rocket science to suggest all five senses are equally touching reminders. Aromas, textures, tastes, climates, and colorful scenic vistas all have the sex appeal to get under our skin—as moving as any poignant song. The point, and there is one, is that both thoughts and things have equal and ample opportunity to shake things up, biologically speaking. Think of a sophisticated stress response finely tuned, well rehearsed, and ready for prime time—we know every part by heart. Food for thought, anyway.

The Physical Nature of Mind

On the periphery of medical science, there's a still fledgling discipline with some objective evidence that mind and body have got it going on. Only an inner certainty could drive the brave souls in neurology, immunology, endocrinology, and psychology to politely tolerate each other and resist the scorn of colleagues in this rather clandestine operation.

A quasi-specialty with as many names as specialists, psycho-neuro-immunology is respected about as much as an *idiopathic* syndrome as it struggles for funding and legitimacy. Yet, as evidence for the biochemical and neuronal communication between brain and body pours in, the mind remains conspicuously absent. The mind is excused because brain is all that lights up the high-tech scanners. In spite of some great work, the discussion circles over brain and body rather than mind and body. Still, it's better than a kick in the head.

The brain's communicator hormones, the protein neuropeptides, have been caught creeping in and around the gut, skin, and blood cells. Shrewdly, these somatic cells have the street smarts to manufacture the molecular receptors required to eavesdrop on any brainiac ideas we may be considering. That means that any serious doubts or sneaky suspicions we harbor will be duly noted by the appropriate organ systems—and vice versa. The entire body politic has the genetic will to alter the dosage of these molecular signals and their receivers on a need-to-know basis.

Additionally, the central nervous system wisely sets up branch offices in the spleen, marrow, liver, and immune hideaways, previously assumed to be handled by in-house operators. This two-way, two level infrastructure of nerves and hormones between brain and body continually briefs and synchronizes the appropriate organ systems.

It's no secret that immune cells learn and remember. Like satellite brains, the blood's white cells chemically monitor and file away all of our public and private associates, while bleeding every nook and cranny informant. Various levels of immune response are conditioned like Pavlov's dog, by the various environmental dinner bells and communiqués. And don't think for a second they're not listening as we speak, to all our dirty little secrets, now and for the rest of our lives.

In these ways, body and brain are enabled to take their responsibilities seriously. They fulfill their communal purpose by faithfully respecting our wide-ranging attention and defending our specific intentions, thus preserving our almost life-like appearance. By remembering and adapting to food and mood swings, the body-brain offers more than better living through chemistry—it does it with electricity.

The Electric Nature of Mind

The extremes of matter are as elusive as mind. Neither is fundamentally reducible to bite size pieces. Sub-atomic events like electrons are not things at all, but energy and information processes which manifest physically as an electromagnetic force. All things have an electromagnetic presence by the nature of their atomic structure, molecular complexity, and degree of consciousness.

Living things being animated as they are, exhibit the most vivacious and lively electrical character compared to, say, the sparkling but exuberantly challenged minerals. Vitality is a product of the organism's orderly arrangement. The design of this energy pattern was, of course, originally intended and remains held by the genetic code.

The EEG (electro-encephalogram) tunes in and picks up the cumulative electrical activity of the highly intricate and convoluted brain tissue. Similarly, heart, muscle, and skin tissue have their dynamic potential revealed in the EKG, EMG, and electrical skin resistance, respectively.

Stranger still, thoughts also exert their presence physically as an electrical impulse. This electromagnetic footprint kicks up the electrical potential of the appropriate brain cell membranes. An informing blip, the charge imparts enough information for the cortical cells to carry out the necessary actions to complete the thought.

Once subjectivity transmutes into objectivity, gangly neuronal circuitry allows contiguous nerve cells to variously alter genetic assembly lines, secrete suitable hormones, and release communicating peptides. The message is then transmitted along precise neural and vascular networks that eventually paint the full mental picture. Alternatively, any change in electrical informational activity in the body/brain is picked up and deciphered somewhere in consciousness.

The electrical signature throughout waking, sleeping, and dreaming consciousness melds into the relatively steady cerebral tones seen on the monitor. The intermittent electrical faults and frequencies during all stages and levels of consciousness are imparted to proper brain cells so they understand just what it is we think we're doing. Body, brain, and mind each take turns at shuffling the electrical deck to jump start all the subsequent bells and whistles.

Momentary hysterics will sound the alarm at the nursing station, while an increasing global awareness quietly refines brain waves throughout the sleep-wake cycles with a coherence, symmetry, and balance. What's more, a fleeting frenzy signals the body to draw obvious conclusions and sign the committal papers, whereas a lasting loving mind-set gives the orders for an integrating, harmonizing, and gracious ending.

Mind Games

The *current of injury* is a sinkhole of electrical potential created by a voltage change in skin cell membranes surrounding an open wound. The negative force field acts as an electrical grid, or ambience, that initiates, guides, and controls local cellular repairs. Then it calls for back up.

Since the neural sheaths along nerve cells are excellent semi-conductors, any electrical signals from lacerating injuries are instantly forwarded to distant immune, endocrine, and brain cells notifying them of the change in plans. In the same way, the informative excitations of all our moods and foods from yesterday were relayed throughout the body and brain for a truly festive dining experience.

This is the same primitive electromagnetic regulation that is responsible for igniting and orientating the fantastic regeneration of amputated limbs in the lowly starfish and the humble salamander. As an underground nervous system, these informed excitations steer the delicate spatial orientation and limb synchronization of the developing human fetus.

This direct current acts as a shocking conference call that connects the mind, brain, and body working in contrast, and in concert, with the slower indirect current via more modern neurons. Just like the fast and slow immune responses, overlapping nervous systems ensure tight controls and orchestration over repair, renewal, and maintenance mechanisms.

Together with the still slower hormonal response of the stress-relaxation servos, all cells, tissues, and organ systems are kept abreast of the state of the union. Once we can pronounce *psycho-neuro-endo-immuno-ology*, we may as well integrate all bodily systems, call it healing, and call it a day.

Now, the majority of chromosomal mass does not code for any known protein sequence, so in our brilliance we've labeled it junk DNA. Imagine that. Recently, the Human Genome Project surprised everyone who cared by finding only one third of the expected number of human genes. It seems we're running out of things to ignore.

But chromosomes, being the single largest bio-molecules, are the most electrically astute. Is it possible that the electrifying personality of these monster molecules might just have something more intelligent to say than what we think of concrete coded language? The remote control of movement and orientation during mitosis and meiosis—production and reproduction—by changing their electric expression isn't just monkey business.

Genetic material is damaged daily by normal metabolic waste, ultraviolet rays, toxins, and random mutations. The local electrical character of the genes themselves, officiates in the routine repair and molecular renewal. It's a good bet that these electronic plug-ins play a vital role in the misunderstood mechanisms that determine and execute genetic expression.

It also seems unlikely that the electromagnetic sensitivity of chromosomes would be incommunicado with the rainbow of radiation from the atmosphere, global magnetic fields, household technology, and the solar flares of our own hot-headed arguments.

Cells learn and remember and the genes are commonly thought of as the brains behind the operation. But if life is going to evolve, something has to the keep the genes briefed on the survival situation. How else are the feeding, mating, and climatic conditions known to these cellular drones, if not through the organism's perception, sensation, and subsequent behavior?

Again, the vibrant cellular membrane serves as the IT middle man that conducts *e*-business between the genes and the immediate environment. Up to the minute levels of physical stress, energy requirements, and mortal fears are electronically and chemically available for nuclear consumption. But it all happens in consciousness first.

Our biological *e*-book of life, therefore, is open to the unfolding chapters of our stressful struggle in an unyielding feedback loop. All of our possible genetic variables are constantly being expressed or suppressed, day by day, word for word, and moment to moment.

Total genome screening is intended to increase the quality of life. By determining each and every inclination to illness, it's assumed that we'll circumvent suffering by changing our lifestyle. But obsessively noting all the innumerable latent genetic foibles we all surely have, will paradoxically tend to fulfill these chromosomal prophesies. That's if we haven't proactively had the preventive surgery. We *already* know which lifestyle offers the best quality of life right now, but we can't seem to live it.

We can't *honestly* cheat in life. The PET scan again reveals how our faces blurt out the tiniest transient changes in blood flow during misstatements to others. Imagine the weary toll on all body cells of the deepest chronic deception—maintaining a lost or stolen identity. The biggest lie we can tell in life is the one we tell to ourselves about who we really are. The physical fallout of this self-libeling is more persistent than any other affliction.

The Soulful Nature of Mind

> *It would be possible to describe everything scientifically,
> but it wouldn't make any sense.
> It would be as if you described a Beethoven symphony
> as a variation of wave pressure.*
> — Albert Einstein

When a linebacker drives his cleats into your foot, specialized pain and pressure receptors in the skin and bone are stimulated—to say the least. A nerve impulse, the action potential, jumps up the spinal cord and over to the brain's sensory cortex. The electrical signal then flicks a switch releasing the precise neuro-transmitters to tickle the brain cells representing the foot. Then somehow, somewhere a painful experience confirms that the game is not going well.

The neuro-chemistry happens in your brain, yet you don't have a headache. The throbbing is mysteriously projected and perceived down inside your shoe. Being a real pro, you'll continue to play with a broken arch, oblivious to the pain that will patiently wait for you outside the lockers. Thankfully, pain is a subjective phenomenon, so you can fashion the final ruling on the flagrancy of the foul—rather than the referee.

Similarly, the sun usually rises in the east. If you're an early riser, the morning rays land on the retina inside your eye. This kindles the optic nerve to fire the information onward and upward, igniting the suitable cells in the visual cortex. A picture-perfect postcard is brilliantly displayed by the excited but strangely darkened dendrites.

Again, the neuro-physiology happens inside your skull where there is no light. Just like all physical sensation, the sunny image is curiously projected back out east, onto the horizon where it's warmly welcome. The fabulous morning glory remains beautifully indirect and open to interpretation, given the value and interest in the eyes of the beholder. The sensational display appears to be exactly where it is.

When a tree falls in the forest, it disturbs the surrounding air. All meaning is lost unless someone who recalls the echo of falling trees is there to interpret the vibes. From within the soundproof cranium, the resonant ruckus can be recognized for what it is.

Similarly, the amazing rainbow is in truth, an unimpressive array of colorless electromagnetic waves. Lucky for you in the heart of darkness, these graded energy frequencies carry delightful information that is, by all accounts, understood to be quite golden.

You don't even need the real thing to duplicate this kind of spectacle. You can imagine it. Dreams seem so real because the brain is an equal opportunity employer. The same perceptual mechanisms create the inner pictures whether the information is real or remembered—the feelings are mutual.

The not uncommon phantom limb phenomenon is a medically recognized example of sensation without representation. Limbs and appendages that were lost to amputation, birth defect, or even under anesthesia can hurt, itch, or feel like they're in an uncomfortably clenched or twisted position.

Like a malicious memory, the legacy of a lost leg remains present but unaccounted for by scientific means. Explanations of residual nerve pathways and stumps have not panned out. This *out-of-leg* experience modestly mirrors the more bizarre *out-of-body* experience—the salacious memory of your whole body in a compromising position.

Both of these ghastly annoyances manifest in the same perceptual realm, on the same magnificent scale, as the pain of your swollen foot, the vision of that remarkable sunrise, and the sounds of deforestation. The mysterious nature of human perception is as ghostly as anything else we can imagine.

Now, as you see and touch this book in your hands, the sight of the words and the texture of the cover seem in fact to be where they are. But the look and the feel of the pages are experienced in the same eerie space as the internal sound of the words. The uncanny image at hand is all in your mind. The whole grating experience comes across as surprisingly real and very, very true. You'd better put the book down before you drop it and think about that one for a minute or two.

Body, Mind, and Soul

> *Nothing can soothe the senses like the soul,*
> *and nothing can soothe the soul like the senses.*
> — Oscar Wilde

Aren't you curious to know where you get your information? All perception and sensation is indirect and elusive. Thinking about it, there's simply no way around it. All your experience is virtual reality and all true blue reality is known in this roundabout way. One's unique interpretations do make for some interesting dinner conversations. Just recall the various opinions of movies that you watch with friends and the diverse childhood recollections of your siblings.

The brain organizes all perception, but it is not experienced in the brain. You might gloss over the mystic interpretations of *reality-is-an-illusion* or misinterpret the meaning of *perception-is-reality,* making these mantras seem very cliché. The hard reality actually exists, but your perception of it is far from perfect and your communication not entirely precise. Then again, it's not really all in your mind.

The actual realm of human perception is beyond any land of the brain or state of the mind. The mind-body problem gets shoved back deeper yet, to the essence of senses, into the strange place where all action happens. Imagine an observation lounge in a parallel netherworld, where objects and subjects meet and greet discreetly in real time. Oh there's another realm all right, but its open door policy allows free access and full disclosure—it's the realm of spirit.

Everyday human experience is indeed nothing but genuine spiritual experience. It's as awesome or awful as you choose to perceive. That again depends on how free your choices are these days, your attention to detail, and just how busy you are. The normal and natural experience you're having right now is as supernatural as it gets. The feeble search for absolute spirit or ultimate happiness is scuttled before it begins. You passed it up in the hallway the moment you left the house with all your gear.

Thinking too much can upset the body and surplus sensation often disrupts any thought processes—as if you hadn't noticed. But the communication is not merely between brain and body, or even mind and body. Remember that those objects and subjects are similar things.

The communication breakdown is between the body and the soul. All that mindful chemistry and electricity are physical manifestations of yet subtler energy. All natural sensation is in cahoots with a supernatural entourage. The poor mind is again denied and gets lost in the shuffle, but *soul versus body* is a better class of argument, wouldn't you say?

Your spirited intentions quite often precede you. A *readiness potential* lights up the monitor a fraction prior to your conscious decision to sit down. A soulful intent heralds the physiological response. Similarly, it's usually a conflicted will or attention deficit that precedes any chemical imbalances in your brain or body. To merely blame the body-brain for any hysteria or despondency lets a disheveled personality and a troubled soul off the hook.

Thoughts often come first and the body responds in kind. At times, when a chemical imbalance actually does take the lead, you can't know for certain or to what degree. There are always multiple factors and your interpretation will always weigh heavy. Once again, your meaning of symptoms makes them better or worse.

Similarly, your subconscious awareness picks up information a micro-moment before you realize it. That allows you to confidently finish your sentence as if you knew what you were going to say—or duck before you see the ball coming at your head. You can call it your mind's eye, the third eye, or a sixth sense because language is all we have to convey what we mean about finely tuned perception.

You're finally forced to admit that all symptoms are worse than *psycho*-somatic. Pain has a *soul*-somatic persuasion that is crystal clear. But remember, your *super* natural lessons in love, purpose, and responsibility earn you a certain degree of freedom, even in biology class. This spiritual glee naturally sings out to all your cellular and nuclear family members, reminding them to honor their purpose, take their responsibility, embrace their relationships, and utilize their freedom.

Is That All There Is?

> *You become what you think about*
> *most of the time.*
> — Ralph Waldo Emerson

At the level of the body, mind-body communication between cells, organs, and systems is carried out through physical means. Protein enzymes and hormones, neuro-peptides and transmitters, and the action potentials along nerves are the Morse code of body talk. As a space-time, cause-effect mechanism, it takes time and energy to manufacture, send, and receive the information.

At a level somewhere between subjectivity and objectivity, electromagnetic fields are the technology of choice for mind-body pillow talk. Thought exerts itself as dynamic information that travels the speed of light along digital, liquid crystal-like neural sheaths. This primitive information highway is faster and cheaper with less overhead as it piggybacks on the solid-state, analog nerves. The peptide police show up later, keeping things real.

The subtlest communication exchange, though, is immediate and simultaneous. This *horse whispering* is typically below the level of conscious awareness in the spiritual realm. Just as the brain conducts a coherent e-choir of cumulative cellular voices, a coalescing crescendo of subatomic intelligence sings out *unplugged* for all bio-spectators to enjoy. Meanwhile, the details of all cellular perceptions are delicately cross referenced, in triplicate—for the body, the mind, and the soul.

Now all that nonsense of responsibly experiencing our symptoms, witnessing our pain, and suffering our purpose makes a little more sense. When our awareness calmly and quietly collects in the basin where the ordinary life transpires, then extraordinary changes can occur.

Our knowledge of everything arises in the same wondrous place. Our sensitivity to pleasure and our perception of pain perform in the same arena. Therefore, paying attention with promising intention refines both the biological and spiritual ambience. With this power alone, it's mere child's play to adjust the volume, dial down the intensity, and blow off some steam of the most painful aches. Body, mind, and soul are literally on the same page and speak the same language, as their essence is one and the same.

In this present moment awareness, childish begging can negotiate a more grownup style of prayer. An unconditional trust in healing-as-usual allows the faith that simply honors and abides by the natural mending process. Any deep gnawing strife we've been carrying around is resolved in the instant that we embrace the enemy within. It often takes our darkest hour to finally find the light switch that's been eluding us. By then, the pain knows not to let us alone and with nowhere else left to hide, we're forced to face the music that's been playing all along.

Soulful Savants

The term *idiot savant* comes from the French, meaning the *learned ones in a world of their own*. With very low IQ, savants access computer-like genius in isolated fields of mathematics, geography, music, or art. They're not taught, nor can they learn, but they've been casually exposed to experience that they marginally relate. It's even more curious how savants get their information.

As we might imagine, their level of attention for one select frequency is fantastically heightened at the expense of the rest. They're not really thinking about their subject in the usual sense, nor are they calculating or creating anything. Without significant processing time for the numbers that resonate, the answers are at once picked out of thin air and mindlessly repeated.

In an infinite realm of possibilities, incredibly, the information is already there. With less ambient noise, preexisting fields of public knowledge are mysteriously received without being consciously perceived. Savants are really a modern day fairy tale of mythic proportions.

It's ironic that it takes the intelligence of idiots, the reality of phantoms, and the unifying teachings of multiple personalities to shrewdly reveal the true nature of mind. Sensationalized side effects like visions, premonitions, telepathy, and telekinesis need not distract us from the everyday thrill and exhilaration of our own thoughtful prowess.

Difficulties with accepting the mind as it is, harkens us back to the historical sabotage of many meaningful experiences. Lessons are easily lost when the profit motive is low. Although, even expensive Navy dolphins have trouble getting their point across. With our own savant-like focus, we might instantly appreciate that consciousness displays itself most prolifically when there is no fear, no restrictive identity, and no *self-*consciousness to get in the way.

All For One

The body, mind, and soul mimic the triad found within all of existence. The three-in-one nature of all things is eloquently revealed by the mystic traditions. Physical, mental, and spiritual character emerge from molecular, electromagnetic, and the subtlest energy dynamics. Somewhat like ice, water, and steam, the body, mind, and soul are graded expressions of the same informed energy, speaking the same mother tongue.

The body, the mind, and the soul
  The seen, the seer, and the seeing
    The object, the subject, and subjectivity
      The known, the knower, and the knowing
        The sensed, the sensor, and the sensation
          The perceived, the perceiver, and the perception
            The experienced, experiencer, and the experience

We've already contemplatively conceded that in view of the soul, the mind is kind of redundant. The essential seer can't really be separated from the act of seeing. The original knower is not any different from the actual acknowledging. Sensation is one and the same as the sensor, and perception is none other than the perceiving being. This experiential *place* is actually the essence of a *person* of no fixed address. The age-old triad collapses down to two and we're left again with body and soul, as the subject blurs with subjectivity, able to relate to the object as one.

Now, it's just one staggering step further for a chance of truly *being-at-one* with the world and everything in it. The perceptual image of that burning sunrise is really an *image-in-process,* a process that is identical to the imagining being. Still *in the moment,* the deceptive dyad suddenly condenses into inspirational *oneness*. When the human *imaging-entity* momentarily identifies with the sunny mirage, it immediately dawns that a creator is creating the creation—in spite of what is already there.

When eastern meditative traditions speak about *No Mind*, they haven't completely lost theirs. They simply mean that by putting down all our things and letting go of all our thoughts, we assuredly rest in the one and only, ultimately human, spiritual experience—without giving it much thought.

Consciousness and Wisdom

> *Kindness is more important than wisdom*
> *and the recognition of this is the beginning of wisdom.*
> — Rubin Theodore Isaac

To be conscious means *"to know."* Consciousness is energetic information. Different levels of consciousness allow different degrees of knowing. Consciousness expresses itself as the self-organizing, cooperative, and creative dimensions of material, living, and thinking things. Knowledge is power because consciousness is responsive—as if it's alive.

Consciousness, with its purposeful, loving, responsive, and free-forming dynamics, manifests itself through endless levels of unfolding displays, as more and more information and energy bursts forth. This precision is expressed in the continual evolution of matter, microbes, plants, and animals.

At the material level, the information is energetic enough to sustain a structure and a functional design. Throughout the spectrum of bacteria, plants, and animals, a primordial sense of interiority progresses through an early prehensile phase, to a basic animal apprehensive ability, and on toward an early primate comprehension.

This emergent irritability, impulsiveness, instinctiveness, and sensation are the early equivalents of us knowing what we're doing. Eventually, from some primeval self-awareness, the human self-reflective consciousness arises for us to know that we know what we're talking about.

This truth about consciousness transcends both the sentimental projections and the arrogant denials of any intelligence *out there*. Indeed, all the way up and all the way down the evolutionary chain, untold information and energy is constantly learning, invariably expressive, and always impressive. Our fear of death is a denial of the very life energy that informs our present consciousness that continues to exist after we die, however modified without the constraints of the body, the brain, or the mind.

The history of life is the history of genetic consciousness that is constantly learning from conscious organisms. That means that the evolution of species via genetic mutation is not entirely random. The genes perceive and respond to environmental pressures with *adaptive* mutations through the perception and response at the organism's level of consciousness. Simultaneously, the surrounding microbial and plant life are taking everything into account as species evolve interactively as the environments for each other.

The universally shared consciousness of everything is like a greatly informed spirit in the sky, remembering the earthly trials and errors with brilliant efficiency. The parallels between phylogeny and ontogeny—evolution and personal development—mirror this same successful learning process.

As consciousness slumbered to its feet, it was fast enough and smart enough to outpace the achievements of millions of years of evolution in a few short years by creating lots of toys and trinkets and civilizations. The higher learning required for cultural evolution saved even more time by not waiting for any brainy genes to mutate.

But the power to speed things up also created some displeasure as we began interfering with the environmental intelligence that helped get us where we are today. Now that human consciousness has effectively outgrown its biological restraints, the freedom to recall its essential cooperative and responsible nature remains to be seen.

Intelligence becomes wisdom when we use information wisely. Profound understanding requires the clever discernment of experience in context with all the facts. As adults continue to learn, a coherent and constructive dialogue of wisdom-for-the-ages can emerge. As the intuitive part of nature, we can consciously tune in to the same consciousness that creates and sustains everything else. The mystics refer to this knowledge as *direct* insights into the nature of reality—as opposed to the *indirect* sights we perceive with our senses.

After all is said and done, we won't find any precise origins of the universe, a definitive time of the creation of life, or an exact emergence of the human mind, because there weren't any. The essential information and energy has been there all along. Long before the beginning of time in the empty space that space now fills is the fullness of an unearthly reality. Once upon a time, there has always been this ceaselessly amusing, lighthearted, and high-spirited playground for all to enjoy if they take the time—and find the directions.

* * *

Inclined to Believe

You don't have to remind me just how strong childhood conditioning can be. To this day I can't go in an elevator without hearing the theme from "Get Smart." If a helicopter is in the vicinity, I automatically start humming the theme from "M*A*S*H." And every time I take out the garbage, I'm Oscar Madison singing the theme from the "Odd Couple." So don't tell me it's hard to change...channels.

Why should I believe in myself when I don't have any lasting opinions of which I'm certain? I had about as much loyalty to beliefs as I had for opinions. If I was always going to be growing and changing and learning new things, then I assumed my interests, values, and beliefs should constantly be replaced. It made sense for me to drop a belief at the drop of a hat if it didn't work anymore. I prided or kidded myself on being a spiritual free agent, but still I wondered about one massive conviction that somehow allows and includes all the others.

I never really believed in anything with all my heart. Not that I was a nonbeliever; it's just that without adequate information, my firm beliefs were shaky at best. But I envied how honestly people came by their beliefs. I was jealous that others became so convinced, contented, and functional with them. In that feeble way, I respected all beliefs.

I never really left religion because I never really joined. I gave all religions the huge benefit of my doubt, assuming them to hold the world's wisdom. The information had to come from somewhere. But I determined that if religious people weren't the nicest and most knowing people around, they must be doing it wrong. There seemed to be as many thoughtful intelligent people who didn't buy into a formalized faith. All I knew was that the truth about reality was incredible and unbelievable, and that this was it—and that's about all.

I had a little trouble with the strong beliefs of others. Conviction always sounded like they were already guilty. Then there was all that sinner stuff.

Give me a break. Work with me here, fellas. I'm already trying to be a good person—maybe the scriptures mean that we all have a long way to go. The fear of God was even a more foreign and confusing concept. I'm already afraid of everything, thanks. I'm quite sure that religion is supposed to be about love— maybe they meant awe. No, I never found the need to take a heavenly father literally. I assumed that the word of God was a figure of speech or a figment of the imagination—but still somehow, true enough.

With all the fighting and animosity around the world and around the neighborhood, I wondered seriously if beliefs do more harm than good. Now, entertaining a belief seemed to me a little more reasonable. You know, get to know each other, see if we have anything in common.

It's the mystics across all times and traditions that have similar inspirations, see comparable truths, and tap into the common core of all religions. Great spiritual masters say that the experience of God is more important and truthful than any conceptions about God. This insider information was apparently hidden from the mainstream for centuries because the secular masses just wouldn't understand. I thought of religious teachers in the same way as my public school teachers—they weren't explaining things clearly enough for my way of thinking. I was just going on a gut feeling but I had the skeptical sense that all of religions and schools had a lot of things to answer for.

For all my pissin' and moanin', my weak wondering didn't do too much damage to my inner life. Deeply and emotionally, I always knew and trusted in my heart that illness was not punishment from God and that life's circumstances were not some karmic payback for past-life misdeeds. You couldn't convince me that life was not ultimately beautiful and that every person was not somehow inherently supported and welcome to play.

I realized that my public charade of shame and embarrassment was kind of a put-on as I took on the role of the contrary son and enjoyed playing the fool. I hid a smirking lack of personal guilt, even from myself. In all my confusion and considerable conflict, I felt that some part of me knew what I was doing—as if there was some demented method to my madness.

I believed life to be either poorly understood by most of us or badly explained by most of them. Rationally, yes, I was missing the instructions and a couple of screws, but I believed I was loved and rather lovable in some universal sense in spite of myself—thank God—and Mom and Dad.

The Meaning of Belief

Beliefs create biology.
— Norman Cousins

More often than not, the preconceived notions we have about health belie our own experience of purpose, love, responsibility, and freedom. Indeed, only a strong will and a stubborn character could hold to harmful beliefs that deny the healing power of love and freedom. What God-forsaken insights do rugged individualists think they're using to pooh-pooh any ideas of spirit? As much as we use the mind to deny the mind, we also use our spiritual experience to deny spiritual experience. You see, even the happy naysayers have a hearty purpose to thank for secret of their success.

Our hardwired sense organs only tune into a limited range of the natural spectrum of light and sound. Insects have the ultraviolet advantage and snakes infer by infrared. Whales keep in touch with low frequency sonar while bats are ultrasound-tastic. We have a knack for taking what little corner of reality is afforded us, then using our beliefs about life to distort and discard much of what's left.

Beliefs variously act as rose colored glasses, stained glass windows, or the painted panes of a business gone bust. Our comfy old positions help to filter out any new evidence to the contrary. They reinforce our need to be right and allow us the pleasure of thinking that we haven't been wasting our time. But our level of interest in life and our rate of return in health are both pre-approved by these great expectations.

Beliefs, cleverly enough, always seem true. That's why we hold onto them so tightly. Initially, our inherited views seem worth fighting for, but as sure as eye color they lose their true blueness with age. Because they're so strongly given and naively taken for granted, we're largely oblivious to the secret wheelings and dealings of indoctrinated ideas. The self-fulfilling power of beliefs gains strength by virtue of being buried and deeply ingrained. Immersed in a hellish world of familial and cultural conditioning, we often don't have a snowball's chance.

Yet, normal psychological development demands that certain stances continually change. Like Santa, the Tooth Fairy, and the Stork, our interest in childhood foods, entertainment, and recreation naturally adjust with newly arising perceptions, values, and beliefs. Looking back now, our beliefs ceased evolving together with purpose and freedom as our views slowly hardened, choices became limited, and our lifestyle settled in for the long haul. Yo, check out those prime-time cartoons, man.

Once we have them, our thoughts are immediately in the past. Rigidly holding onto our sacred old ways keeps us living in it. Naturally then, our present experience is often pre-judged by past memorable encounters. But realize that even recollections of the good old days are embellished or diminished by current beliefs. More importantly, our possible future growth and learning are falsely, blindly, and prejudicially hindered by unyielding convictions.

Common beliefs about illness and aging impose undue stress and unfounded fear, no doubt denying a fair defense and reasonable repairs. Luckily, the body itself doesn't worry so much. Cellular certainty and biological instincts can provide compensation for even our most stubborn ways. A particularly robust and stoic physique may just eek out a long and mean-spirited life in spite of the nagging beliefs of its caretaker.

Doctor in Latin is "*docere*," meaning to teach. But "*to doctor*" also means to tamper with or falsify. Physicians and healers can rise to the occasion as altruistic menders of disillusioned belief by example and education or fall into the habit of manipulative demi-god by default and denial.

The Placebo Phenomenon

> *Use the medicine as much as you can,*
> *before the people stop believing in it.*
> — Sir William Osler, MD

The history of medicine is the history of the placebo effect. Up until the modern era, most medicine worked, until the majority believed it didn't. Even a healthy percentage of patients today respond to sham treatments with a trusted decrease in symptoms.

As a well-accepted medical phenomenon, the greater meaning of the placebo response is still largely missed. The name alone is a demeaning projection in the preservation of professional authority. The word *placebo* is derived from the patient honestly trying to *please* the doctor. Or worse, it's an attempt by doctors to *placate* the patient.

It's considered a costly nuisance, almost an affront to medical science, when up to eighty percent of people respond positively to a bogus cure. How dare subjectivity interfere with objective science? Non-believing specialists are begrudgingly forced to grant the patient's expectations some minimal import—except with respect to their own particular specialty, of course.

The placebo effect has followed a path of any worthy artifact. First, it was denied and ignored, then it was controlled for, and eventually it was studied in its own right. Still, the bang and the boom of modern gadgetry detract from any real respect for the poor thing.

The official take-home message of the placebo phenomenon is limited to the legal realities of marketing drugs. It's an expensive hoop for drug companies to jump through—vigorously controlling trials so that synthetic pills perform better than natural sugar. But don't cry too much for them, as the cost is naturally passed onto the true believers. Curiously, no one seems to get excited about the healing power of sugar.

All that the ethics committees can make of the placebo encounter is the unethical deception of innocent patients, denying them informed consent. Barring a profitable *placebo pill* (one that biochemically engenders trust and faith in the healing relationship), bid a fond farewell to any deeper meaning of the placebo experience— and welcome the birth of yet another cliché.

On second thought, if we could find a personality to blame, maybe someone could conduct a study. Given the many personality-associated illnesses and histrionics, the placebo personality was naively believed to be the naïve, gullible, and weakly willed patients. Of course, that meant ignoring the complaints of strong-willed problem patients who pester nurses, refuse doctor's orders, and ask the most questions. They tend to do better.

Just a little more inquiry and we might notice that beliefs are working most effectively *right now* in people with no symptoms at all. Their trusting optimism is not as helpful in creating illness in the first place or hindering the healing in the second place, as with the cynics.

Conscious beliefs are intellectual opinions about our personal experience. But less-than-conscious beliefs secretly *construct* the perceptual framework of that experience, by faithfully honoring one's hidden identity in purpose and love. The subsequent strain on the body is even less apparent.

All treatment invokes the placebo response—the more dramatic the treatment, the more theatrical the response. That's why blue triangles and purple ovals vie for top spot in the pill industry. Beliefs have a hand in everything from subtle energy therapies and bodywork to the electrical saws and hand drills of orthopedic surgery. A placebo response is the product of the expectations and trust of both patient and provider. Their belief in each other and the cure itself create an environment for both the herbs and the bone chisel to be effective—allowing innate healing to finish the job.

It's funny that the placebo response happens even though the patients *know* that they have a fifty-fifty chance of getting goofed. Patients eagerly consent and sign up for the drug study and so does the doctor. Nobody hopes that the drug works more than the sweaty pharmaceutical rep with the indigestion.

Imagine secretly enrolling both patient and doctor in a mock research study using *only* a sweet placebo. Absolute belief that the treatment is a real one, one hundred percent of the time, we might just account for the anecdotal stories of spontaneous healing, inexplicable recoveries, and surprising longevity.

Let's say a legitimate medication works seventy-percent of the time with a placebo response of thirty-percent. When we're actually sick and taking the true tablets, we're never quite certain whether our improvement is because of the pill's seventy or our mind's thirty—the eventual healing is the same.

Similarly, we can't be sure that our psychotherapy helped because the technique was genuinely effective, or because our relationship with the therapist was trusting, supportive, and convincing—or that for the hundred bills an hour, we'll damn well shape up. In the same way, the time off work, the respite from family, and the nourishing nurses may just give the old healing response as fine an edge as the surgical blade.

The placebo effect, of course, can't overcome massive doses of powerful drugs. But admittedly, even by improving the timing, dosage, and delivery systems of insulin and other hormones, we still poorly emulate the precision of our inner pharmacy. Also, we can expect fewer side effects when the body uses its own in-house alchemy—like none. Even in long-standing ills that require aggressive therapies, the patient still has to want to recover—and there's no pill for that.

Morphine works its magic only because it fits the cellular receptor of the body's endogenous endorphins—the chemical fun behind the natural high. Drugs can only work by locking onto molecular receptors that are already prepared—awaiting the body's home-made version. When the body does it, perhaps nobody is sick, no one is notified, and nobody gets paid. Sure, the body's pharmacy can be fatigued, aggravated, or bankrupted if reckless food and drugs overwhelm the body's stores—but there it is.

The healing power of belief isn't any more unbelievable than the potions, lotions, and notions that we swallow from multi-level marketeers, late night infomercials, and every corner health store. We're not talking about some *magical* belief that creates a kind of supernatural healing. Rather, the experience of love, will, and freedom simply sanction the superb natural healing to proceed as usual.

When certainty and meaning overcomes doubt and unfairness, healing can happen. No matter the cause, cure, or condition, a deeply moving revelation can shatter the most long held assumptions. Then a truly healing experience is the most gratifying, the most helpful, and most possible.

A faithful healing ambience creates the same trusting atmosphere that assures little Janey that her sniffles will be gone by morning—that she'll be able to play in the big game tomorrow—if she *intends* to. Parents have a small window of opportunity to condition the young body-mind for a lifetime of good faith. Being rewarded for recovery instead of for sickness, Jane won't need to use illness to get out of school and get out of chores just to get her parent's attention.

The power of suggestion, especially with kids, is as strong and as real as all our beliefs to the contrary. But again, there is nothing that parents can really do. The best *wellness aura* that Mom and Dad can muster is the one that naturally radiates from their current beliefs—which nobody can deny or examine for them.

Mom and Dad's unassuming air shines with the same light as the uplifting radiance felt in the doctor-patient relationship that quietly awakens a patient's healing response. The multi-tiered and multi-talented communication within mind-body-soul allows for all healing mechanisms to be receptive to the meaning perceived in the symptom and the treatment alike. When we finally let up our resistance and put down our defenses, we invite normal biological resistance and natural immune defenses to take up the appropriate arms.

Ultimately, the placebo response is *not* an isolated phenomenon in its own right—nothing is. Instead, the pleasing event represents a tentative and foggy view of the tip of a life-sized iceberg. The massive and slippery notion is that attention and intention powerfully influence the tension below the icy surface. It's no wonder that the blood tests and x-rays rarely match the patient's complaints. Somebody might actually have to take care of that guy.

All healing is ultimately self-healing. Even after they've de-bulked the tumor and irradiated the cancer, we're on our own. The blind faith in conventional medicine and the false hope of alternative medicine eventually gives way to our own *knowing* faith and *active* hope in the true healing power of purpose, love, responsibility, and freedom.

The Nocebo Phenomenon

> *We do not see things as they are but how we are.*
> — Talmud

We're about to enter another dimension, somewhere beyond belief. Welcome to placebo's evil twin—the *nocebo response* is the placebo from hell. It's the fulfillment of feared and unwelcome suggestions and it's happening all the time. The very mention of side effects in clinical trials produces the same rashes, blurred vision, or constipation from the colored sugar as from the legitimate prescription. And again, patients know they have only a fifty-fifty chance of getting the real deal. Incredibly, even *anti-*nausea medication can be made to *induce* vomiting with the precise dose of comedic irony.

Side effects are the unwanted, but wholly expected effects, of partially treating a whole person. We minimize them by pretending they're *on the side*. But we never know if it's the remedy itself or our jittery attention to warning labels that upsets our stomach. The legal cautions required on medical devices are intended to inform the public and decrease liability, but no doubt act to increase the side effects—and the law suits.

By all accounts, bad news is more valuable, entertaining, and profitable than good news. It's just business, but no one can escape the massive ground swell of negativity that bombards air waves and daily newsprint. Statistics and surveys are decimated and overblown, spewing out dangerously biased shrapnel of suggestion. The crumbling cynicism and pessimistic aftermath proves indeed that things are mostly bad and can only get worse. Fear-mongering sadly serves the hidden agenda of *especially interested* groups in need of sympathy, support, and funding to cure their affliction.

The clashing, baffling, and alarmist public warnings can drape a person's awareness like a voodoo death curse to reap the same grim results. Maimed and disfigured factoids drive misplaced dread and despair into people's hearts. Broken heart deaths like hysterical pregnancies and paralysis are not just cinematic scenes, but the living realities of stillborn beliefs. A non-violent purse snatching can actually kill Grandma a few months later, not unlike the shocked and traumatized war veterans suffering vague and mysterious syndromes.

Medical students tend to forget all the diseases they endured under the second year suggestion when working half asleep and sleeping half awake. People will even die on cue. They'll hang on until a meaningful anniversary or let go on the day of the professional's premonition—pleasing to the end.

Cultural doom and gloom creates oppressive clouds of anxiety, depression, and blame that needlessly darken the individual's outlook. Our likelihood of proving the statistics correct depends on our relationship with all the grief. Terminal and incurable labels are of no help to the possibility or the quality of the singular life. While statistically correct, these intellectual pearls tend to suck any hope or peace out of the final resting environment.

It's still commonly believed that progressive physical deterioration and debilitation are inevitable with age, while a lifetime of youthful exuberance and vitality is naïve and incredible. People actually prepare for the worst by slowing down, taking it easy, and retiring from life. That's why it behooves parents, teachers, and healers to become serious leaders on the frontlines of health rather than comical cheerleaders on the sidelines.

The brilliant power of the nocebo effectively proves the greater possibilities for the placebo. While the placebo allows a general healing environment, the nocebo fashions an incredibly specific although undesired symptom. Given the hypnotic suggestions of our own running narratives and the hue and cry of family and peers, our work-a-day life may well become specifically undesirable.

This hypnosis is, by all means, self-hypnosis. From within or without, the power of attention is brought to bear on a feared but believed intention. The mass hypnosis of cultural conditioning is somewhat inevitable. But without the hysteria, care can be taken to deal with the havoc.

Personal beliefs about human nature might now be considered a little more seriously, given the added family significance. In a true healing experience, the victim is always the spiritual victor, no matter the physical fate. Taking responsibility for our health includes appreciating and examining the conditioning effect of all our beliefs.

Health and illness are not as simple as positive thinking or as trivial as negative thinking. But incessant mental imprinting works behind the scenes to slowly bolster or bewilder the body's intelligence. Of course, certain body types show an amazing tolerance for unbelievable torment. Placebo or no placebo, if we're not paying attention, we can still walk in front of a bus.

The Nature of Nurture and the Nurture of Nature

Any argument between nature and nurture dissolves in the mix of the mind-body debate. In the meantime, our throw-away views about genes and environments directly determine our method of parenting, patient care, and politics. Believe it or not, these hardened opinions are largely responsible for the nurturing nature surrounding our dinner tables.

Convinced that human behavior is all in the genes, we're a natural to bribe, punish, and coerce. At best, we think people don't change and there's no point in rehabilitation. Things stay the same and this is as good as it gets. At worst, we assume the worst in people and gentle eugenics seems reasonable to skim the algae off the old gene pool. Teaching and preaching personal responsibility, we stand for strong work ethics, strictly enforced moral values, every man for himself, and pulling up bootstraps. If those in our charge aren't listening, we may have to take matters into our own hands.

Human goodness with this set of beliefs is believed to come only from a forced repression of our primitive evil nature. Of course, innate loving-kindness looks like childish idealism when humankind looks like a selfish gene machine, struggling to survive at all costs. With this kind of headstrong purpose, we can surely elbow our way through a long and outwardly successful life. But in the end and in the extreme, it's a purpose without much love.

Somehow, somewhere the naïve among us assume the social environment to be more decisive in all human manner. At best, the cracked bureaucratic windows down at Worker's Compensation and the Unemployment Office just need some more red tape. At worst, people can't do anything for themselves, all criminals have hope, and nothing is completely their fault. By the time we're hearing the cabbage crying as we cut up the coleslaw, we've already ordered the red paint to throw on the furriers.

Through these well-intended eyes, human evil looks like suppression of an essentially sweet nature that got extinguished long ago during a terrible tantrum. Human nastiness is simply a perversion imposed by unruly dictators during the tender years. The fragile young soul has been beaten, badgered, and betrayed beyond anything it could control.

The job of healing the world with this set of beliefs is going to require a multi-cultural response, expensive social programs, family interventions, and basically, lots of counseling. If nobody's listening, we might have to go on a hunger strike or hang from a tall building. Watching a child go through normal growing pains is too much agony to bear, so there's little choice but to love them to death. When inexplicable hardship strikes someone like this, it makes us wonder about too much love without much purpose.

The middle way starts looking pretty good about now—except that it's not in the middle. Reconciling extreme beliefs requires a vision that encompasses both. This puppet-master mentality finds balance in the strength of purpose with the softness of love and a mature responsibility that is free to create. A meaningful politics embraces the nature of nurturing and the nurturing of nature.

Complex human behavior can't logically be pinned on nature or nurture alone. Like mind and body, both nature and nurture are personally interpreted. Like emotion and sensation, nature and nurture remain subjective perceptions of objects in consciousness. Naturally, anything that nurtures freedom and responsibility while guiding purpose and love is a good way of teaching, policing, and caring for patients—not so difficult to believe.

Now, not surprisingly, identical twins are *not* identical people. Fascinating and fabulous, normally conceived cloning just doesn't get the fanfare that unnaturally scary cloning does—maybe the twins need more picnics. Genetic manipulation will always be more publishable, patentable, and profitable than consensual procreation—well, on second thought.... Regardless, the sovereign identity rules the roost for genetically identical people.

Nothing shows the moody nature of genes better than identicals with opposite temperaments, interests, and talents. This incredible flexibility of psychological possibility can be appreciated by imagining the many paths not taken in our own lives. Appearances are often deceiving because attitude and behavior are motivated by identity and belief more so than family disposition, dollars, or DNA. Genes then afford us a realm of possibilities rather than prescribing the limits of our destiny.

The primordial nurturing of fetal twins in the same womb might be responsible for the psychic resonance seen in the incredibly parallel lives of twins living apart. That early amniotic ambience would seem to have the strongest conditioning effect on development, one that endures for the rest of their lives. Rather than taking sides in the nature and nurture debate, we're sort of climbing inside to simply admit that our subtle nature is more powerful than our obvious nature and more profound than literal nurturing.

We know the reality of good and evil because Hollywood tells us so. In feature films, digitally re-mastered mythology portrays the same heroes and villains with which humanity grew up. Except now it's literally projected for ten bucks a pop. While we're absorbed in the celluloid fantasy, it's easy to forget that the cops and robbers are also a figurative projection that reflects the opposing forces within our own embattled psyche. Afterwards, back out in the street, like a camera flash that we can't blink away, the evil force seems to be lurking in each passing shadow.

Gradually, we're subliminally recruited as unlikely action figures in our own epic life story, now imitating the art that's been mimicking and mocking us all along. This rather uncouth and uncultured conditioning is woven into our now twisted minds, escalating our tangled and wicked webs.

Of course body chemistry affects behavior. Nobody will argue that testosterone doesn't induce aggression in animals and humans. But barring any injectables, it's our civility and our patience that determines whether we release the rage at the gym or by kicking the dog.

The most insidious evil, however, is the ignorant belief by everyday folks that evil is a natural force in itself that somehow popped into existence with the genes of human beings. This legacy repeatedly instills the fear and fulfills the fantasy in successive families like a generational *lazy Susan*. As a vulgar human invention, evil mushrooms in the darkness of unenlightened minds. Remember, there are no bad personalities, just extremely mushed and mangled ones.

Both our personal disposition and genetic predisposition can be stimulated or stunted, flourish or falter. The motivation of our behavior is physically pressured by genetics, food, and the climate—our things. Our genetic possibilities are variably and conditionally expressed through the persuasion of personal, familial, and cultural consciousness—our thoughts. The body and the society provide the material scaffolding for our developing consciousness, while our conscious identity and the cultural setting offer the emotional backdrop for the hilarious high jinks around the gene pool.

Recognize that both our nature and our nurturing provide the environments for each other, co-habitating and co-evolving, just like everything else. Human behavior, then, is an expression of our experience in purpose, love, responsibility, and freedom that naturally comes from nurturing—no matter our nature.

* * *

Inventing a Lifestyle

I've been changing my diet, exercise, and lifestyle every year since high school. It often looked like I was flitting from one fad to another and following one fashion after another. But I wasn't leaving one thing for another—I was adding one thing to the next. I like a regular routine more than anyone, so if I kept changing, it's only because I was forever finding out new stuff—but I'm getting tired of it.

With my meso-morph build I could really do some damage at the buffet. As a kid, bedside piles of dirty dishes blocked the morning sun. Put it this way: mom never complained that she needed a garburator. I had no weight concerns or body issues, didn't even know what that meant, and everything was well with the world. By my mid-twenties, though, my runaway appetite was catching up with me. My reckless eating program would be difficult to shake.

I was no natural build, though. There was always some guy who looked fit and happy without much effort. My thighs ached and felt like lead if I didn't lift something heavy everyday—like get out of bed. I needed vigorous workouts if only to have a somewhat pleasant mood. Any fat tendencies were kept at bay for the time being.

Exercise never took any willpower for me and it was always a total high. That is until life would rear its ugly head. Any mild injury, inconvenience, or opportunity to grow up could easily knock me off my sacred little routine. After a few weeks, my half-happy disposition soured, my normal urges ceased, my body seized, and my appetite exploded. I felt my precious world spiraling out of control and panic would set in.

And gaining weight was not easy. It was punishing work, force-feeding pizza and beer until I could barely stomach it—but I was up for the challenge. I knew the real meaning of no pain, no gain. Only after a long and miserable tantrum was I finally left to get the ball rolling again. But the damn fragility of the whole thing was ridiculous. I needed a life. Luckily, getting back in shape was always easier than expected. My muscles remembered the way, and I couldn't believe that I had whined away all those months.

What may have appeared to be yo-yo dieting was really yo-yo despair. I lost weight naturally and easily when I finally crawled back to my normal life. I quite enjoyed eating fresh wholesome food and I was at a loss to explain why I couldn't always live the way I most enjoyed. I played dodge ball with the same 20 pounds for years before finally tiring of it.

Being a little over-fat was not as uncomfortable as always being full. Plus, I could carry it pretty well. But the same two hundred and fifteen pounds felt great on the way down, and life-threatening on the way up. The state of the body and the look of life could feel totally different at the same weight.

Of course, I was guilty, embarrassed, and self-conscious even when I was fit and trim. I didn't want to stick it in their face or make others feel badly about themselves. But mostly, I was ashamed that weight was still such an issue for me. Just like I couldn't be the playboy or the boyfriend, I couldn't be the jock or the nerd. Maybe it had nothing to do with the weight or the girls; maybe it was me.

Besides or because of these conflicts, my initial interest in living healthily was inspired by this first-hand experience and how much it affected my life. Before age or illness made me care about aging or death, I just wanted to think clearly, get up the stairs, and do up my pants.

I learned more about my body from yoga than I did from all the books, courses, or patients. Nothing was as impressive or dramatic in changing the technique, goals, and enjoyment of everything I did. Even by the age of thirty, both gravity and mass tend to flatten out the lower back and round out the upper spine. Gluteal muscles then become atrophic—guys lose their ass. I knew the body was responsive, but still I was blown away by just how much mindful movements could recover posture, range of motion, and muscle mass. The incredible increase in hip motion and stride length made simple walking a newfound pleasure.

Granted, I was too excited about the physical changes to understand yoga's higher purpose. But boy, I'll tell you, the yoga bodies sure looked smoother, sexier, and more naturally balanced than the hard bodies down at the gym. Nevertheless, I could appreciate both.

Meditation turned out to be that vacation of a lifetime. It was my opportunity to let go of all my tiresome schtick and pretend for the moment that I was the person I knew I could be. Slowly over many years, I was putting everything I had learned together, if only in spurts, and began to get an idea about the *meaning of a healthy lifestyle. I became just as comfortable visiting the yoga studio as the gym, the meditation retreat as the holiday spa, and the Catholic mass as the Jewish temple. I realized that when ultimately it's all the same thing, for the same ultimate reasons, then it's all good.*

A Meaningful Life

You are what you think about what you eat.
— Jane Roberts

The biochemistry of how and why serves to strengthen or weaken our physiology—no matter what, when, or where. The way we use treatments and go on retreats, take supplements and tonics, and engage in all manner of eating and exercise, reflects how responsible we are with our freedoms. Indeed, our purpose and love create the biological underbrush in which all caring and curing must struggle. A body-mind of conscious calm and persistent cool is far more beneficial for health than all the heroic efforts against aging and illness.

As important as nutrition, fitness, and lifestyle are for vitality and well-being, they can't account for the happiest, longest lived, or healthiest among us. The habits of contented centenarians are all over the map—except for moderation, adaptation, independence, and decent relationships. And they don't usually have hundred-year-old parents. Common symptoms can be significantly tweaked by how we behave, but the social and cultural leftovers are not so easily burned off.

The good news is that—done in *the spirit of health*—diet and exercise can nudge our consciousness toward freedom, awaken our faith in love, and ignite our passion for purpose. We might just tailor some alterations in those faded old genes or sew the seams of that tattered persona.

The same advertising giants that brought us *"If it tastes bad, it must be good for you"* and *"No pain, no gain,"* also brought us artificial sweeteners, fat blockers, and exercise-in-a-bottle. Young America has been getting fatter and slower ever since these brainstorms hit the coast. Epidemic, recalcitrant, and nonrefundable obesity are authentic side—and rear—effects of faux fitness, fake foods, and the false promises of our friendly neighborhood health and fitness industry.

To be sure, those infomercial hard bodies and fitness models didn't get that way using goofy gimmicks and God-awful gadgets for five minutes a day. Any kernel of truth in these comical ads is inflated and flouted as the next panacea. *But you'd better call right now as this offer—and the results—last only as long as people buy into it.*

Old notions about the largely framed and unfit masses reveal the mistrust we have about the body's intelligence and distorted ideals of what health really looks like. Within reason, one can be hale and hearty while pleasantly plump and tremendously anemic with a 32-inch waist. Both fearful waifs and fixated full-figures have related food issues in variable bodies. The *spirit of fitness* would have to include the soul of the person.

More meaningful than our present size and shape is how and why it happened to get that way. The body will naturally assume its most suitable and artful design when it's not hindered by our awkward assumptions about its nature. Alternatively, the rivers of fear and denial eventually wear down the most rigidly enforced Adonis.

An unhealthy balance easily topples any sacred lifestyle regimes, especially when relationships and careers are sidelined by a solemn fitness routine. Like any aversion or obsession, overplaying the healthy habits often represents the inflamed passions of lost love—it's motivated by fear. Think of this psychic pushing and pulling as more vigorous than any circuit training and more harmful than the bench press is helpful.

Oxygen, water, and food all give us life—and they can take it away. In the right dosage we can combust, drown, or merely blow up. Food is simply the weapon of choice in the love-hate battle within our bulging defenses. But eating rises to the level of dining, and workouts take on a sophisticated finesse when purpose, love, responsibility, and freedom make them meaningful.

The Purpose of Food

> *A healthy person eats what is served.*
> — Buddhist aphorism

When we eat with the sole purpose of losing weight, virtually any diet program can work. But if the *meaning* of excess adipose remains, it's only a matter of time before the fat bounces back. Even our svelte new form isn't strong enough to lift our old tubby self-image. Obesity is indeed an incurable disease when our purpose is incorrigible. The body lives to fulfill our beliefs, not necessarily our dreams.

Man cannot live on bread alone. Food can never satisfy one's highest needs and usually inflates the lowest ones. When disgust with our appearance is the main motivation to lose weight, then our attention sticks to the fat—and vice versa. Alternatively, when behavior is driven by loving something else more, the healing journey is self-sustaining and the unwanted flab slips beside the point.

The battle of the bulge correctly implies that we've made enemies out of our food and our fat. When emotions and cravings highjack our freedom, then sadness and lust make all our food choices and we really end up fighting ourselves. As senses are neglected and bodily cues dulled, hunger and thirst grow insatiable. Gradually losing our wits, a consuming desire overpowers a now meager will—and the groceries seem to be eating us. What is the purpose in that?

Even for those honestly concerned about health, at best we eat to prevent illness and feel energized. But more often than not, we gorge to celebrate affairs and glut to finalize breakups. We imbibe to honor friendships and suffer loneliness. We're forced to entertain customers as much as cravings. Comfort foods feel good going down—not so good when the guilt and the gas come back up. Then, of course, we eat to treat ourselves for a job well done and punish ourselves when we screw up.

The purpose of eating rarely comes up, even in the face of indigestion and regurgitation. But a healthy relationship with food insists on knowing why we bother. The need for basic nutrients and sustenance are generally not a problem in western society and not particularly helpful for a discussion about purpose—we gotta eat.

The purpose of eating at the level of the body includes sensual enjoyment. By sampling a variety of colors, flavors, aromas, and textures, we honor our sense of civility by stimulating, balancing, and honing the senses.

Eating is elevated to a loving gesture that counters cravings and eases the appetite. Eating to sharpen satiety cues and lessen stress, we then also enliven our vitality and our will to live—not bad for a sandwich.

Never mind the reinvigorated healing response and soothing sensitivities and intolerances that a well-meant diet can offer. The physiological pillars of sleep, menstruation, elimination, and digestion can be deepened or lightened and heated or cooled as needed. We haven't even mentioned fiber yet.

Tasty trials and tribulations with likes and dislikes, both common and exotic, keep us in touch with eccentric needs. Without starving or snacking, we'll find meal times a lot more momentous. Taking food wisely might just educate our dim-witted habits of that second cup, third helping, or fourth round. Most importantly, a hearty balance of nourishment releases our bondage to food by freeing the shackles of our awareness.

Dining literally rises to a ritualistic communing with nature. Taking our place in the energy cycle as an active member in the food chain endows us with a certain respect and gratitude for its cooperative perfection. Breaking bread and building bonds, eating can also be enjoyed to nurture the family and community.

It's important to appreciate where food comes from, what it originally looked like, and how it got here. Admitting and accepting responsibility for the violence of catching, killing, and preparing the food gives our primitive nature some subjective release. Beyond the intellectual interest in the food's storied past, we might also defuse any pent-up animal instincts from exploding over the fence and violating the neighbor's Rottweiler.

Even more, it might dawn on us how cultural ignorance fuels the violation of ecosystems and species toward the depletion of nature's bounty.

Oh yeah. The happy little side effect of eating on purpose includes an abundance of energy and prevention of the occasional illness. Now, if we could just lose our taste for that greasy kid stuff, we might be getting somewhere. When our food values become more than food labels, our body will thank us.

The Love of Food

> *To eat is human, to digest divine.*
> — Mark Twain

Our actual eating values are exposed by how we eat. Busy being busy with more important things, we eat fast food fast. Convenience food cons us out of any care or concern. We're content with pre-mixed, pre-washed, and pre-cooked food. Better yet, TV dinners, pick up, and delivery do it without dirty dishes. Soon, we'll be asking for pre-digested food. *Would you like fries with that?*

Anticipating our next meal, our next course, and our next bite, we have little time to enjoy what we're chewing. Eating too fast to taste the food, we become rather tasteless ourselves. Arguing, reading, driving, and watching the soaps or the news—God knows what people do while they eat.

We need these distractions, though. It helps us ignore the discomfort of a flushed face, sweaty brow, bounding pulse, runny nose, and tightening waistband. But without listening to these biological screams, we can't get any satisfaction. We can't be satisfied with what we don't really need and we're not getting what we need because we're not paying attention.

If we miss the honest pleasure of a good meal, pure physical exhaustion may be all that's left to stop us from finishing what we started. When we make an art form out of mindless eating, we eat more calories that are less fulfilling. Then, *stopping when pleased* remains a distant memory of infancy, when we happily fed until a contented burp told us enough was enough. Now guilty, stressed, and stuffed, we'd be happy and lucky if the whole disgusting mess passed right through.

Animals metabolize a finite number of calories—then they die. Rats on a high nutrient, ultra-low calorie diet can live up to twice their average life span. But for all our genetic similarities, extrapolation of mammalian research is always precarious. The little rodents don't harbor our depth of insecurity. But the theory that metabolic exhaust fumes accelerate aging and disease doesn't mean we should live a caged, ultra-sparse, and ascetic existence. It means that the mindless over-consumption of anything is more exhausting and life-threatening than the mindful enjoyment of everything.

Nutrition means *to nourish* and is related to nurse—meaning *to care*. Mindful eating is thoughtful and careful eating. Slowing down the pace of eating, we can afford to pay more attention because we pay less for the processing of the drive-thru fare. Imagine the crispy, crunchy, chewy moisture of each succulent bite and the sweet wafting aromas from palatable presentations, garnishes, and niceties. With a little refinement of the taste buds, we might even harbor a guess at the subtle herbs and spices.

Of course, before we can taste the food, we need to chew it. Mother was right about enjoying the bite, the chew, and the swallow. Since a majority of taste is mixed in with aroma, we may want to stop to smell the rolls. But if we butter, salt, and sweeten before we even sniff the buns, the soup, or the coffee, then we'll never know what the stuff actually tastes like.

We can't develop a taste for the original sweetness of oats if we've never tried them without sugar, milk, fruit, and syrup. Food actually had some flavor before it was "prepared." But if we try our food before we treat it, we'd have to admit that our favorites are favored because of the fat, the sauce, the cream, and the topping.

The love and care of homemade meals creates a warm and loving environment that enlivens digestion and assimilation. Turning mealtime into a ritual sacrament, we'll absorb the good intentions, the reverence, and the meaning along with the nutrients. If that's too hard to swallow, just recall the contentious, demeaning, or abusive dinner table that turns our stomach, ruins our appetite, and upsets our sleep—*that* we believe.

Even the nutritious value of so-called health food or junk food is somewhat determined by how it's eaten. When we eat with reckless abandon, the most wholesome food is indigestible and left for dead. A gentle, happy gut, on the other hand, makes the most out of the least nutritious food. When we let loose our constant anticipation and release any reservations, then we bring new meaning to the phrase *free for lunch*.

As we listen and trust our own inner wisdom, we can ignore the confusing and conflicting expert advice. For the love of food, we can eat whatever we want.

Responsible Eating

> *More people die from overeating
> than from undernourishment.*
> — Talmud

The hoards of diet gurus, programs, books, and magazines are enough to drive the most fervent granola cruncher nuts. News and literature are littered with half truths, biased sources, and ridiculous ads. Governments and schools use calories, carbohydrates, and cholesterol to create a frenzied, fat-phobic society. The fear of food is worse than the food itself. We all know what a healthy diet is—we've just never seen one.

Fats, carbohydrates, and proteins all come out looking pretty bad from one study to the next. Since there's nothing left to eat, we're forced to invent food substitutes. Reducing food to isolated chemicals, we do senseless things with them and meals become meaningless. The synthetic sweeteners, feigned fats, and genetically modified proteins are necessary only because real food has lost its value and availability. Then the staggering arrays of diets swagger in to make things worse.

The bottom line in the food industry determines our bottom end. Shelf-life and marketing are responsible for our chosen shelves and markets. Production, processing, and packaging serve the company's interests for the most practical and cost effective way to feed the masses. When foodstuff is sold alongside hardware, it's a good bet that the nutrients are in line with the nails. *Got iron?*

The eventual harm of additives, preservatives, binders, fillers, flavors, and dyes will be argued forever while science awaits the objective deaths. The point right now is that these chemicals alter the original taste of the food. That's why we need so many artificial condiments to add a dash of simulated flavor.

Removing the care and concern from our diet, we remove the food's value. When we milk the isolated facts and fads to nourish lowest common needs, we create new and improved foods that are *lite* on flavor, *low* on taste, and *reduced* in meaning.

The shelf-life of packaged entrees is longer because the food is basically dead. Processing knocks the living daylights out of food by degrading its given nature. To appease public outcries and legal compromises, long deceased wheat flour has its ashes enriched with the cynical toss of a multivitamin into the mix. Our bodies know full well that the live symphony of nutrients is essentially silenced.

Then the baking and fattening of the white doughy marvel ditches any last hope that soluble fiber will stem the tide of blood sugar, weight gain, and future insulin dependence. However, by confusing real carbohydrates with damaged and dying ones, the so-called *carboaddicts* can rationalize their bizarre excuse for *"just saying no"* to those evil apples and oranges.

Strangely enough, there's no such thing as bad food. Like people, the only evil food is that which is impure, adulterated, and unloved. Carbohydrate as a predominant energy source is fine before it's refined, sanitized, and simplified into baked nothings. Aggressive processing decreases the grain's satiety and nutritive value, while increasing its obesity and diabetic value. The bittersweet topping is the denial that reducing the food value has anything to do with lowering our values.

Protein is essential unless it's animal, mineral, or made in the lab. The majority of grains are already being genetically modified and people aren't dropping dead in the streets. It's not that these and other food by-products are so dangerous or terrible—it's that they cost more and they're worth less.

Fat is vital for hormone production and vitamin absorption, but lethal if it's hydrogenated and otherwise *trans*-formed—never mind how they aerosolize it. Cholesterol is not the killer we're told it is until it's tormented by the stress of being processed or burnt; not to mention the guilt in eating it. Make a mental note that cured, smoked, fermented, pickled, and preserved foods are pre-aged and pre-stressed for our convenience—*will that be for here or to go?*

Granted, the original nutrients are retained in bottled, canned, and frozen food, albeit in some altered state. But a simple comparison with the vitality, color, texture, aroma, and taste of freshly prepared food plainly shows that purpose and love is more than the chemical constituency of the specimen.

The pesticides and herbicides in fruits and vegetables, like the antibiotics and hormones in livestock, are of concern, though happily sanctioned by government and medical officials. But as smoking and now second-hand smoking have readily taught us, we needn't wait for objective *horrendomas* to appear on the x-ray. These injected and sprayed chemicals are simply not food, and therefore retain only their business value.

Even working among overcrowded, unnaturally fed, and abnormally fattened bovines isn't enough for the abattoir attendants to consider vegetarianism—unless they're paying attention. But their bodies collate all the pertinent details to hold silent vigils later, as need be.

The rapid growth and fiery metabolism of kids helps them get away with eating just about anything. But we've got to wonder if they'll soon get caught, now that food is virtually plastic. Teenagers are already showing signs of imbalances previously reserved for adults, like high blood pressure, diabetes, and heart disease.

The good news is that the humungous amounts of salt, fat, and sugar in all the cartoonish foodstuffs are not nearly the worst of it. Worse than the physical ill-effects of near-food on children is the life-long conditioning of outrageous cravings, emotional instability, and the spinning attention span of a purpose, love, responsibility, and freedom gone wrong.

Ain't Nothing like the Real Thing

> *Following any diet is spiritually poisonous.*
> — Buddhist aphorism

Real food has got to be good for us. What an incredible concept to have fresh, homegrown, pure, whole food. Nature's buffet includes an incredible variety of fruits, vegetables, beans, grains, nuts, seeds, herbs, and spices. Recognize anything? Chances are we wouldn't notice rice, almonds, peppermint, or vanilla on the side of the road, fresh out of their natural habitat. It's funny that just like bad people and bad news, really bad food is believable while really good food is often a fairy tale.

It's a crime what a ransomed cliché we've made out of whole food. We have the legislators to thank for the legal meaning of the word "*whole.*" As long as a whole grain of anything was seen somewhere on the floor sometime during processing, flour has the right to boast a whole wheat label. Of course, since it's already ground into flour, there's not a whole lot of anything there. That's why bread needs all that preservation just to survive the night. These days, the chances are good that the average stomach has never met a whole grain of anything that didn't upset it.

Grains of wheat, barley, rye, and oats actually come from the ground as hard little kernels. Like whole seeds, vegetables, and beans, they provide the perfect percentage of food energy and a precise complement of nutrients. The time and attention for longer cooking is included if we buy the full value-added package.

A well-balanced diet literally balances the colors, sizes, and shapes of food. Plants directly access the sun's energy and have developed the most protective nutrients against harmful radiation. Absorbing various light frequencies, the corresponding colors of nature's candy cover us with the continuum of specific protectants. And there's infinite pleasure in enjoying the diversity of edible species. Species? Remember biology class: kingdom, phylum, class, order, family, genus, species—real food is actually alive and well at one point.

Then of course, a wide range of tastes, textures, and aromas promise the perfect proportion of carbohydrate, fat, and protein. The potpourri of prospective nutrients helps round out the needs of the mind, body, and soul.

Each step in food processing harms this nourishment while helping the food industry. The vital punch of organic food is also stymied, once it's packaged and preserved. And because we can never be sure exactly what we're getting, it's a good thing to remember the placebo effect when buying everything else at the health food store. Calorie counters, food scales, and nutrient tables should start looking pretty silly about now.

Forget about checking labels, because real food doesn't have any. The avalanche of energy bars, protein shakes, and organic snacks feature all the right buzzwords and numbers to make us think they're actually wholesome. But if the "health food" has expiry dates and *shifts during shipment,* it's not healthy food. Better to spend our time growing, preparing, and shopping than memorizing fat grams, calculating calories, and weighing out portions—our body knows all that stuff.

Whole food is wholesome because it retains its essential purpose, love, responsibility, and freedom. A spice's purpose resonates as the information in the original structural design. The loving nature of veggies is in the electromagnetic vitality that carries the memory of their growing conditions, how they're prepared, and the devoted intent of the chef. Fruit bears its responsibility in its heartiness and robustness—the genuine shelf-life—rather than its dye job. And finally, the freedom of nature's salad bar awakens our own primordial freedom by its bountiful assortment.

These nutritional dynamics are literally fit to be eaten as sensitive reminders to our innate, if not subdued healing force. Real food is the most valuable because it's the most nourishing, integrating, and purifying for all levels of body, mind, and soul. Biological filtering systems and defense forces need this vital bolstering for the inevitable load of toxins and impurities we inhale just walking out the door. Life is, after all, a fatal condition .

Imagine the ultimate non-diet as the Low Faux Diet (LFD). Even meat, chicken, and fish can be fresh, whole, and relatively unharmed. We'll likely lose our taste for canned, ground, and meaty by-products once we start adding a dose of reality to our plate. But don't be surprised if many of us forget about meat all together. Without the spices, the gravy, the beer, and the barbeque char, muscle is about as tasty as squid tar tar. If the full-bodied texture of meat is indeed satisfying to the taste, it's only because the rest of the diet has no consistency to speak of. At least there's the social aspect of tailgate parties and summer grilling.

Vegetarians get a bad name because "*vegetarian*" is a bad name. The term doesn't do justice to the various mixtures of fruits, beans, grains, nuts, seeds and spicy delicacies. A vegetarian can go a year without eating rabbit food. Those who eat less meat enjoy fewer hormones and antibiotics with less reconstituted and regurgitated solar energy. The accumulated toxins that work their way up the food chain make eating meat almost like sleeping with every cow that beast has ever slept with.

Don't forget the refills. Except that at this gourmet buffet, we're so satisfied by texture and taste, so relaxed from aroma and color, and so endeared by the company, we'll eat surprisingly less and enjoy it a lot more. When we've honestly tasted the freedom from food, it's all we *care to* eat.

This anti-diet satisfies the food requirements for virtually every disease and condition. The prevent-everything diet, the diabetic diet, the cancer diet, the blood-heart-stroke diet, and the obesity-depression-pain diet are all indeed the Low Faux Diet—more or less. The inflamed gut may have temporarily lost the capacity for real food, resisting the resistance and all. But slowly and gently with carefully cooked and strained food, the innards can regain their balance and recall their purpose. Disease and discomfort have a way of serving as harsh, if not tardy, reminders for us to live the way we were meant to all along.

The societal obsession with supposedly healthy food is itself another fear-based eating disorder. Just watch the eyes and manner of health nuts who feverishly stick to eating all the right stuff. Their angry defensiveness often reveals that they don't necessarily *have* all the right stuff.

Juggling all the dubious nutritional advice takes the balancing act of a balanced persona, referring to the food-borne wisdom that's been there all along. In this day and age, it's impossible to eat exclusively real food. But knowing what real food actually looks, tastes, and feels like we can sprinkle it generously on whatever is served. This could be the start of a beautiful friendship. When shopping, preparing, and chewing our food ceases to be a chore, then we'll have the habitual hankering for fresh wholesome food and be glad to clean up.

Any treats we desire on the LFD are freely allowed without guilt or dyspepsia. Appetite and sleep slowly return to follow the sun and season, free from alarm. When salivating over the multi-grains, dried fruits, mixed nuts, fresh herbs, and spices down at the bulk bins, just remember—they've got cameras in there.

The Purpose of Exercise

As hard as it seems to stay in shape,
it's easier than shaping up your emotional and spiritual life.
— Gary Ratson

It's not nice to fool Mother Nature. Our body knows why we're loitering around those co-ed gym palaces, how we're sustaining that six-pack, and what we're avoiding at home. The fluorescent tights are hot and the body waxing is tan-fastic. But what force of will maintains that trimness at those twenty-four-hour nightclubs? Exercise is counterproductive when motivated by hatred of body fat, the fear of aging, or the evasion of the old ball and chain.

The body mass prays and pleads to model itself after our beliefs. That makes our triumphs only as enduring as our faith is true. Since most physiological effects wear off within weeks, that treadmill of torment keeps us playing catch-up in more ways than one. A longer running reason might just ease our pain and change our attitudes about exercise.

Muscle of one type or another largely defines the medical meaning of fitness. The long and the short of fitness are strength, flexibility, lean body mass, and cardiovascular competence. Sport science has come full circle by shrinking its preventative health advice down to a modest thrice-weekly session of brisk walking. Anything more is medical overkill, obsessed recreation, or some other deviance.

Even this moderate amount of exercise is enough to bolster the biomarkers of aging such as blood sugar control, temperature regulation, bone density, percentage body fat, blood lipids, and the rest—but who's counting? The body will take care of itself when we take care of our purpose.

Now, when the meaning of fitness is reduced to the muscle, its purpose is limited to body. Realize that elite athletes are not icons of emotional health, while pro football players compete for the shortest life span. Because more often seems better, no amount of machismo is enough for the muscle heads in the weight room.

More physical training would indeed be better if it wisely embraced mental and spiritual fitness. The flexible parameters of aging mentioned above are further tempered and more easily maintained when sport is used to lessen emotional and spiritual strain—and there's no end to that. A washboard stomach and buns-of-steel are merely extraordinary bonuses.

The value of exercise goes beyond burning calories, toning muscles, jumping higher, and running faster. Physical activity is vital for burning off the stressful chemicals. Besides cooling our jets, a revved-up metabolism appeases the appetite and procures the appropriate playing weight. The exercise-induced normalization of sleep patterns, digestion, and elimination all reinforce the body's defenses and steady its homeostatic controls—preventing or restoring needless imbalances.

The ease of inhaling and exhaling our full lung capacity is not merely exhilarating; it's a good sign of longevity. The joy and buoyancy of swimming up stairs and dancing up storms hardly needs a degree in discipline. By finely tuning our bio-feedback, we skillfully detect early signs of illness, sensitivities, and other discrepancies.

Ironically, the greater our sense of motion, the more our body will never cease to amaze. It's the beginning of trust in the body's quick responsive loyalty. The purpose of exercise can't be impressed strongly enough—it's the same higher purpose as everything else. In the end, it's an end in itself—there is no finish line—it's the love of the game—and all that jazz.

The Love of Exercise

*One mindful repetition
is equal to ten mindless ones.*
— Arnold Schwarzenegger

It's supposed to be painful and boring and we're well prepared. We're wired for sound and raging with 'roids. Our munitions belt is loaded with walkmans, beepers, and cell phones. Maybe we should get a hand-held global positioning system, just in case we can't find the toilet.

Remember the books and the magazines, charts and tables, heart rate monitor and fashion headband—don't forget a pencil. The bottled water and energy bars are mandatory because the water fountain is twenty feet away, we've got ten minutes on the incline bike, and haven't eaten since brunch. To be fair, all the mirrors at clubs do make the jaunt to the can look like an obstacle course.

We must be doing something right, because like everyone else, we're red faced, suckin' air, and none too happy. We're cheating like crazy, dropping weights, and mumbling something about monthly debits. We'd like to get that workout done with and basically get the hell out of there. Most of us do too much too fast, ignore proper technique, and invite injury—a thankful respite. Don't bother showering, there's no chance of meeting *the one*.

Mindlessness is easily illustrated every Friday night. When we have a girl or a guy or a party in mind, we can forget about work, forget about homework, and forget about getting anything done at the gym. The weights feel like lead and our legs feel like rubber. When our mind is elsewhere, we're no good for no one.

Now, if we collect up all the toys, turn off the telly, dial down the disco, and throw a towel over the digital display on the stair climber, we might have something here. The flashing calories, mileage, speed, and time are eventually as useless as the wattage and $maxVO_2$—this isn't the Olympic trials and you're no Mark Spitz.

If we're paying attention, we can put down the pen and paper routine. We'll remember our reps and adopt our routine by heart. It's best to get into the habit soon. As internet monitors take over the gyms, we'll end up with a cyborg physique to match our virtual love life.

With every move we make and every breath we take we naturally create the optimum rhythm to follow. The body keeps track of the precise duration, distance, and intensity to sustain. A true target heart rate aligns with the flow of the breath, the coordination of the muscles, and the confidence in the joints. The joyfulness of a full breath is not labor intensive and the gracefulness of moving steadily is without strain. By trusting and adjusting to any displeasure of the muscles, breath, and joints, we'll gradually improve to greater fitness levels without the harsh training conditions.

Mindful exercise is a completely different animal from the inside. Only a keen eye can spot our slight smile, the look of certainty, and pure exuberance. Our well-honed attention follows a line of sight along the full range of joint motion, feeling the muscle from origin to insertion. In this way, we invite more muscle fibers to contract in the primary movers and dismiss those cheating secondary shakers. Attention to form, alignment, and breathing lessen any extraneous contractions.

The patience required to tackle the controlled kind of tension in exercise is good practice for facing life's uncontrollable strain. Befriending the muscles we never knew we had is essential if we don't want them holding us up behind our back. We can rightly leave the gym early because tripling our efficiency cuts training time, reps, and resistance by half. Working the largest muscles catches the smaller ones and covers the nebulous ones. If we don't leave the gym with more energy than we came with, then maybe we're doing something wrong.

Now, when a pitcher takes aim, his pitching performance is taken for granted. The arduous hours of practice make certain that the fundamentals are not lost on the body. With complete faith that the muscles and joints will accurately deliver, his trusting attention is purely and squarely on the catcher's mitt. It's this same belief in biological precision that allows us to concentrate on wherever it is we think we're going. Beyond winning and losing, trusting our body through these moving experiments teaches sport's greatest lessons for living. The next time we sink a putt, knock down a pin, or hit a home run, we might realize that the truth about *being-the-ball* is out of our hands.

We can carelessly walk through any yoga, aerobic, or spin class. But the body knows if our heart is in it. Muscles learn quicker without the mixed messages in the music, magazines, and three-in-one maneuvers. When we pay the body the quiet respect it deserves, it responds to our demands by side-stepping injury and stepping up enjoyment.

Lost in the rhythm of our heart beat, foot steps, and the passing trees, we might just find ourselves out standing in a field. This moving meditation entices the runner's high, tempts the oneness of the mountain climber's peak experience, and allows access to the pro athlete's zone. We can't get these experiences in a pill and still get to work the next morning.

The adrenalin junky and death-defying daredevil are both fun at parties. But these extreme sportsmen and women symbolize the massive repression of the spiritual peaks that the majority of us are afraid to climb. If we could touch heaven during a simple walk in the park, we'd realize how the denial of physical passion creates our depression while watching the Ironman triathletes and our sarcasm in seeing the Eco-Challengers—good onya, mate.

Lasting learning for mind or muscle requires enduring intention and focused attention. Pure physical pleasure and emotional delight are the heavenly side effects of this vigorous will and grace. With a little imagination, we might just charm this corpulent creation into a little soulful recreation.

Responsible Exercise

> *It's not over until it's over
> and even then it's not over.*
> —Yogi Berra

There is no ultimate training program or universal fitness routine. Not to worry though, the fitness industry is busy making it up. Gyms won't make money if everyone shows up and athletic stores would go belly up if the equipment actually changed lives. That's fine because there's no room at the club for all those life members, and the place would stink. The business plan for fitness is based on the fit getting fitter and the fat getting further behind.

The endless load of fitness books, tapes, and courses show what a bust the fitness boom has been. We should at least receive a marketing degree. TV infomercials are in the middle of the night because we've got to be half asleep to buy into passive motion machines, electrical muscle stimulation, and spot reduction creams. If it slides under the bed, folds up into a suitcase, and works while we sleep, then it's probably not exercise. We didn't believe in the placebo response but we believe that rubber bands and rolling balls can reduce that gut.

Muscles don't move with the same intentional vigor when external machines or electrical pads are the primary movers. We have to pay attention. Somebody said, *"Nobody went broke underestimating the intelligence of the American people"*—and there's another one born every minute.

Most fitness gadgets and gizmos use distorted truths of rehabilitation therapy. Electrical stimulation and passive motion prevent muscle wasting, bone loss, joint contracture, and blood stagnation after injury, surgery, and plaster casting. Now, if we're walking around with any of these problems, then maybe calisthenics shouldn't be a priority.

The body is not the complete moron we're led to believe. Try training on a treadmill and then running at the same speed when hitting the pavement. It's not going to happen. Muscles remember precisely every pace they're put through. That's why the best training looks exactly like a specific sport—and is called sport-specific training.

The enjoyment and benefit of exercise depends more on our attitude than on our wallet and the exact piece of equipment. Real exercise, like real food, is the least expensive because we're not paying for fancy packaging, high-tech production, and plastic ingredients. Walking, running, climbing, dancing, stretching and lifting—just add gravity. Or water. *Whatever floats your boat.* But don't just do it; mean it.

We don't need an expert to tell us to do things we love and try things we don't. Pushing and pulling at every angle of major joints strengthens every muscle and releases imbalances. We never need more weight than we're already carrying around, so by using intelligent angles and creative views we won't even need a gym. Ever wonder why they call them dumb bells?

Genuine cross-training is about all the same angles, speeds, and intensities that concern all the muscles and joints. With muscle fibers running madly off in all directions, it takes quite a variety of activities to catch them all. But we'll prevent overuse injuries, sagging imagination, and the harassment charges from salivating over the fluorescent tights.

Skill-dependent exercises like cross-country skiing display the same catch-22 as getting a job. We can't get into a good position until we have the skills, and we can't get the skills until we assume the position. It's hard to fall into the zone when we're worried about falling off a cliff.

Fitness often seems like a metaphor for the unfairness of life. Until we achieve a decent level of fitness, workouts surely suck. They're ineffectual, boring, and embarrassing. It's difficult to find any rhythm, coordination, or competence. Without much intensity or endurance, we're not burning many calories and hitting the wall is reduced to stubbing our toes.

We just can't get our groove on until we're already fit. Impatience will have us quitting this round of resolutions before that ever happens. Plus, we look ridiculous and everyone is staring. It's not long until we're emotionally bruised and demoralized, that rubber tire is annoying, everything hurts, and sweating is itchy. We can't feel at home at the gym until we're at home in our body. Oddly enough, most people blame exercise itself for this memorable but crappy experience.

If we can persevere for few months, workouts become more effective, enjoyable, and easier. By then we've lost a couple pounds and bulked up a few fibers so we might actually burn a mouthful of calories. The outfit's not feeling so tight anymore and we're doing most of the staring. If we can swallow the idea that purposeful movement is a natural act, then exercise may just become a piece of cake.

Soon enough, muscles feel invigorated by the gravitational pull, leaving us energized with an out-of-this-world confidence. We breathe deeply but easily, knowing this as our birthright. We were flexible enough at birth and we can be again. Groceries now seem to lift themselves and for some unknown reason, we decide to start making the bed.

Conditioning our skeletal muscles affects every organ system in the body. We can tell because we're sleeping through the night, feeling our first hunger pang in years, and not clearing the room with our body odor, bad breath, or natural gas. Everything works better and runs cleaner.

Even after a week of the flu, we're up and running as if being sick was a welcome time out. The muscles retain a memory of their own, so getting back into shape only took a month after the three months of therapy for the back that we injured while making the bed.

With all that, we're nicer to be around and other people don't seem all that bad either. Maybe we'll quit that job, take that trip, or start that course. If nothing else, we'll be supportive and respectful when loved ones are inspired to change. Mostly, though, the air smells fresher, colors look brighter, food tastes better, and cartoons are boring.

If we can tweak or awaken everything that still works, old injuries and chronic annoyances become less bothersome. By deriving pleasure in our physical being, we can proudly reclaim those unsightly bumps and resistant bulges as amusing trademarks.

The typical exercise-induced exasperation is a symptom of mindless exercise. Anticipation of distant results makes it impossible to find any point in the immediate misery. But the patience, perseverance, and optimism for getting over the hump only happen with a change in perspective and profound shift in purpose.

Exercise may be mostly about muscle, but muscle is more than size and strength. Strength is related to resting muscle length, leverage, range of joint motion, and cellular size and conditioning. But in any given condition, mental intensity and focus are the most important for power. Furthermore, the metabolic effects of training are most gratifying. Our metabolic set point gets a boost from an increasingly conditioned percentage of lean body mass that uses more energy than the slow-going flab. We actually *do* burn more calories while we sleep when our muscles are alive and kicking.

Mindful exercise teaches us where our muscles are, what they do, where they want to go, and how to get there. We learn that by giving our muscles, joints, and bones what they like, the longer they'll take us where we'd like them to. Mindful exercise enjoys the present moment no matter how far we have to go, how long we've been away, or how far we've come—it doesn't matter what exactly we do.

Exercise stresses the body in order to easily handle our daily distress. On the other hand, meditation calms the mind to maintain itself during hectic times. Both the self-inflicted stress and relaxation have been shown to slow the aging markers to enhance vitality and well-being. Fitness from outside in and inside out—using the body to please the mind and using the mind to ease the body—what could be better than that?

Yoga means "*to yoke*" or unite the mind, body, and soul with everything else. Yoga is the true life-specific sport, as it calmly conditions the mind to stay focused in the midst of activity, mimicking daily working conditions. With deliberate awareness during demanding activity, we learn to keep our head while everyone around us is losing theirs. When we bring our undivided attention to sports, home, and office, we honor the living yogi within and recognize it in others—*Namaste.*

Exercise reminds us to keep it moving, meditation reawakens our youthful imagination, and yoga recalls for us how to play like a child. Unlike someone trying to relive the good old days, our mindful activity merely honors them in enlightened ways.

The word *art* in Latin is "*artis,*" meaning to join together. The art of fitness, like the ancient Martial Arts, is the integrative conditioning of the body, mind, and soul. The art of medicine seeks to ease the early imbalances along the way to physical, emotional, and spiritual fitness.

The word *religion* comes from the Latin word "*re-ligio,*" meaning to reconnect to that which has been forgotten—something like remembering, experiencing, and identifying with the truth, beauty, and goodness within and without. It's beginning to look as though medical, physical, and spiritual practice may well be identical siblings—poetic or medical license notwithstanding.

Jog Your Memory

> *It's déjà vu all over again.*
> — Yogi Berra

Recall that all cells learn and remember. All tissue responds to exercise and all body cells communicate in one way or another. Because of its mobile nature, muscle is the first and most obvious responder. Like big contracting nerves, skeletal muscle's highly organized and innervated structure has a very lively electromagnetic character. Brains and brawn are more closely related than the muscle heads would lead us to believe.

It all started with the micro-tubular proteins that act as both mind and muscle for single-celled microbes. As proto-muscles, they provide the punch behind the bacterial movement needed for feeding, fleeing, and reproducing. These primitive cyto-skeletons also act like mini brains by allowing for the trial and error feedback memory loops that are necessary for adapting and evolving. Like quantum level pipe organs, these tubular bells resonate with the intention and attention of primordial inner life.

We might think that human cells should have the best pipes, but this cellular savant-like prowess goes all the way down. Each cell of each species all the way up the evolutionary chain is endowed with this memorable brawn. Even our brain cells have similar structural elements to remember their responsibilities and maintain their freedom. We might owe an apology to those behemoths at the gym.

Like in the human brain, cellular memory isn't stored in the protein or the fat of the muscles, but leaves its particulate remnants. Just as past experience is alive and well and living in the present moment, so all that muscular activity in the gym is locally logged and filed for future reference. Coordination, technique, and natural ability are remembered like riding a bike. That explains how after injury or lay-off, we don't have to start back at square one. Muscles are not so thick as to forget how careful or careless we've been, how much we enjoyed the training, and how much we cursed them.

Our smart-ass muscles are also plugged into the rest of the body. This electrical communication allows all that bumping, grinding, humping, and pumping to immediately influence our moods, choices, and behaviors. Prior to the slower conventional training response, this electronic media keeps mind and body up to the minute.

Whether we're learning at the cellular level or the college level, this biological freedom of information is the original shareware. Muscle then re-creates itself, along with our bones, joints, and skin into our own self-image so that eventually we begin to look like we feel. The tensions and constraints within our identity take shape as the contortions and tightness in postural muscles. Given our personal preference and fiber composition, specific muscles and bones will bow to the pressure of our twisted and resisted psyche. It's enough to give us a headache. But to be fair, with the agility apropos true love and freedom, muscles can also take it easy, stretch out and relax with the proper instruction.

We can hide for only so long because love it or hate it, our personality reveals itself in our posture and facial expression. Those youthful laugh lines lay the foundation for future wrinkles, just as we intended. Over time, all our joints, bones, and internal organs get the message, scrunching down and skooching over just a bit. Realize that this is over and above the accepted genetically programmed deterioration. At least now we can understand that our tight-lipped, tight-wad, and tight-ass friends all mean well, doing the best they can under the circumstances.

Our ancient inner scars gradually become as visible as external injuries, but from deeper wounds. Psychological baggage is like a knight of darkness that is hopelessly brought to bear in a defensive posture of body armour. Now remember, these used to be voluntary muscles. We can't consciously relax them anymore because we've mindlessly locked the door and left the keys in our subverted identity. This troubled tonicity joins the already anxious stress response and gimpy healing response that we *do* know about.

Human touch is vital to human life in more ways than one. A baby's growth and development are literally stunted without a loving touch. Nobody denies how warm hugs and hot hands can ease a pain or lighten anxiety. Now fast forward to the forlorn and weary adult wearing the same tired old skin and bones. Deep-seated memories of trials and traumas have worked their way into frozen joints and restricted muscles, now literally cold to the touch.

Wise healing hands have, since ancient times, massaged and manipulated the skin, muscle, and joints to open the lines of communication. The various therapeutic body workers literally jog the sedentary memory while helping us find our keys. Occasionally, touching emotional breakthroughs and moving spiritual revelations can happen, no less believable than the self-inflicted highs of any deeply stirring activity. Top secreted information is now consciously retrieved and perceived in a new light. The energy can now be transformed into something more productive than a sore back.

We can credit the therapy, the healer, and/or the patient, but they all came together when mutually prepared to create the trust, expectation, and healing ambience that recreate and enliven a sullen life. Exercise, yoga, and meditation similarly remind muscles of their original supple yet responsive character, allowing graceful movement at any age. In this way, voluntary muscle redeems itself while involuntary muscle (heart, lungs, and gut) comes under a modicum of accomplished control.

Whether stimulating an athlete's *Chi* with acupuncture, an asthmatic's *Prana* with yogic breathing, or a heart patient's *Chakras* with meditation, the well-meaning nudge serves as a wake-up call to the slumbering soul. In the same way, chicken soup serves to awaken a grandson's *Rúach.* We can be sure that this purposely loving energy has correlative biochemical bandits just waiting to be caught by roving scientists.

Synthetic botulism toxin is a recent makeover favorite to paralyze facial muscles in attempts to smooth out the wrinkles above. Consider, though, that these tightened voluntary muscles are already partially paralyzed by the secretly admonished persona. Externally relieving the resistance allows further avoidance and a false impression of underlying skirmish. Ironically, the utter lack of facial expression now says it all.

The cosmetic health professionals are just doing their job by giving the public what they want and exploiting the latest technology. But in this meaningless conspiracy, everyone forgets that like liposuction, hair plugs, and breast jobs, the ultimate happiness lasts only as long as the purpose is deep.

Recall the few distinguished souls armed with a gracious sophistication that literally smoothes out the perception of chronological aging. When their posture commands authority and their voice grabs our attention, then their eyes have the room and all are struck by their glowing presence. That defining radiance blazes brighter than the skin, shinier than the hair, and bigger than the boobs.

* * *

Beginning to see

I guess you could call me a sensitive guy of the 60's, 70's, 80's AND 90's—he says with a straight face. The pain of "not knowing" was always so intense—the constant surface tension over a deep chasm. It seems I was destined to blindly take on the load of ignorance that was blissfully ignored by everyone else.

I couldn't shake my past without literally leaving it, selling it, and giving it away. The three hundred books that I dumped off at the Children's Hospital Book Fair were a load off my mind, as my ego was getting a swollen head. (I bought half of the copies there anyway.) Maybe I would finally get off the pot, if I didn't have one to piss in. It's easier to live in the moment when you literally have no past to go back to. I was never even much of a pack-rat, but I suppose I still have a few bones left in my closet.

It's not that my family circus and circle of friends were so negative; they just couldn't relate. I felt a certain resistance to my self-expression, whether it was there or not. It was simpler for me to excuse myself and return when I had something nice to say. True, it looked like I was running away, but I learned early on that what we resist tends to persist. I had to make peace with my persistent past before I could lull it into a deep trance—and then break its neck. In a way, you could say that I faked my own death, but I wasn't kidding in killing the phony life that didn't mean much to me.

Sure, I rejected the system and left the establishment, but I never considered that they might not take me back. Now, I think I could probably play the game and go through the motions, but I'd be playing by my own rules, and moving to my own beat. It might just be possible for me to embrace society with a clear conscience, now that I've accepted that material reality tends to defeat the purpose of ideal intentions, a little bit.

Now whatever you do, don't follow me. I'm sure I have a few major blunders left in me. But I think I'm beginning to get it, because in spite of no money, no honey, no funny, I'm smiling more brightly than ever before. There's no way I could have peacefully survived a vanishing nest-egg, while enjoying constant rejection, without learning what I needed to know. And although success and failure are now less important than what really matters, I'm a little embarrassed by the minimal returns. Well, you have to walk before you can run, but after this moving experience, I'm more than happy to be wherever I am.

Beginning to Heal

Don't let school interfere with your education.
— Mark Twain

Now, if we could just forget everything we've been taught. To know what health really looks like, we need to know what we're looking for. To know what health really feels like, we need to know what we're doing and trust our experience. When we clarify, simplify, and unify all common knowledge, our own intuitive rhythms begin to sound pretty good.

We've seen that a healthy perspective of well-being comes with the integrity of a mature self-image. That view of health deflates somewhat when we peer through the emotional and spiritual immaturity of an inflated self-image—the puffed-up portrayal of a few select parts

As we're able to watch what we're doing and see where we're going, the meaning of health becomes clearer and more to the point. When we get a hold of ourselves for the moment—our only point of power—we can center our gravity, balance our wits, and keep our cool. This presence of mind extends the endurance to deal with dilemmas of external conditions.

If that's asking too much, or seems a little far-fetched, it may be time to ask what is gained by defending comfy old positions. True, familiarity breeds a certain comfort and definite contempt for the unknown self. But when we proclaim our right to fly off the handle in the heat of the moment, then the well-known self appears to be the more immediate threat.

When emotions get the better of us, then every random action is followed by an equal and opposite robotic reaction, and we reap the recurring grief of some kind of rebel without a clue. Yes, human emotions are normal and healthy, but forever being had by them is particularly dumbfounding.

Ironically, this mindlessness is a curious attachment to the wandering mind, so much so that we lose the flair to use our mind to the fullest—and think for our selves. On one level, we're so full of ourselves that nothing else can get in—but it's fullness of a mind with a false bottom.

Words cannot do justice to the *No mind* experience, which, oddly enough, is the mindful and caring capacity to listen to others, witness oneself, and accept reality just as it is. Pure mindfulness in a moment of *No thought* is a far cry from the absentmindedness of a careless occasion.

We've all experienced the limited *self-consciousness* that creates doubt, hesitation, and second-guessing. A limitless *Self-consciousness*, on the other hand, is a heightened awareness of a higher Self. This is the deeper essence of *just "being"*—the naturally loving, purposeful, and responsible *Being*, with the calculated risk-taking and educated guessing of a free and open spirit.

All our anticipating, postponing, and worrying reveal the false hope, or doubt, in the future, at the expense of current reality. Similarly, anger, resentment, blame, and guilt reiterate a blind faith in the persistent illusion of previous experience—the way we've been so far, up until now. Furthermore, the refusal to age gracefully, like the fear of death, is the real experience of a synthetic self that can't let the past die to the present.

Imagine, then, all our thoughtless lifestyle habits, life choices, and deadly decisions that lead to various mental and physical obsessions, vices, and addictions. For us to invite agony into the future by jacking up immediate pleasures, it would appear that we're trying to escape from some present pain. Except that, in reality, we're running from a *past* that has got its teeth into the *present* like a rabid dog that won't let go.

Similarly, we need to overlook the jealous manipulation, greed, and conflict we inflict on others, if we're to increase security for our insecure selves. Why would we hurt others unless we're scared for ourselves, selves that feel vulnerable enough to take precedence over others? In this *less-than-conscious* state, we truly *know not what we do*, as all our schemes and self-mutilation are not really on purpose—not an awakened purpose, anyway.

So, we're forced to confess that most common illnesses and all excess suffering are due, in part, to the spiritual mistake of an emotionally crippled intellect. At least, this frequent faux pas makes things worse, cramps coping, and hampers healing. But, this uptight outlook goes on to ignite the physiological pressure-cooker that, when mixed with senseless activity, food, and recreational additives, stirs up the bio-chemistry of a very sick joke.

> *"The most divine art is that of healing...*
> *it must occupy itself with the soul as well as the body."*
> — Pythagoras

Diseases are defined under the categories of injury, inflammation, infection, degeneration, or cancer. After that, we're left with various functional pain syndromes and poorly healed chronic conditions. But the common contributing cause and cure of many needless ills are found in the blood.

Helplessness and hopelessness are dangerous as they literally cut off the life-blood of the body. Overplayed immune defenses, schooled by depressive and defensive neurotic forces, dig into darkened vessels. Anxious tensions and angry resistances similarly train the overgrown arterial muscles and overstated arteriole spasms.

The eventually confining sclerotic arteries of heart and stroke disease recall the longstanding emotional scars and limiting values of a blinded purpose. Biological clinginess and cellular adhesions then faithfully follow the grasping of a truly broken heart. A mindless consumption of comforting conveniences offers a compensatory fullness that literally chokes off the life supply with fat gorging immune cells foaming at the mouth.

The inhibitions of loneliness and meaninglessness combine to create the inflamed perceptual stress that adds the caustic inflammatory juices, inhibiting the blood from its appointed rounds. As the flow of life is denied in our experience, a spastic muscular strain literally denies the warm-blooded healing response in all chronically fatiguing conditions.

> *"There is no beginning. There is no end.*
> *There is only the infinite passion of life."*
> — Frederico Fellini

By now, it's clear how we secretly wreak much of the havoc, undermining our best-laid plans. Only by swallowing our pride will we stop eating ourselves up or chewing out others. When we examine distorted beliefs, stent narrowed views, and surrender harmful behavior, we realize that most imbalances are reversible, many are self-healing, and the rest can be eased up or slowed down.

Healing at a profound level asks us to surrender something that is not even real—except our resistance to give it a rest. It's a thought experiment where we drop the charade, assassinate our own character acting, and allow the full light of consciousness to take center stage. Then we return bits of material and pieces of mind in exchange for the peace of mind that refines and redefines who we really are.

The esoteric wisdom traditions use subtle verse to suggest this healing experience, a truth too obvious for exoteric science. This peaceful easy feeling may be like walking with God—or having an angel on our shoulder—but for sure, it's a loving presence and healing radiance that's highly contagious. The gift of the present has the full healing force to lighten the heavy symptoms that arise out of gripping the past and fearing the future.

It's not uncommon to feel badly enough for long enough to eventually feel dead inside. Nothing we undertake really does it for us anymore; nothing grabs our fancy, or sustains our interest. The impression that nothing can light our fire, kindle our spirits, or enliven our passions is the sure symptom of a soggy soul, drowned out by a waterlogged and petrified ego.

Rebirth and renewal are possible, though, if we sink our senses into the beauty of nature and goodness of others, to recall something true about ourselves. The humble charm of animals, art, music, kind acts, or heroic feats, strikes a chord that already runs through us and resonates with an essence that is already there. Once we re-cognize the soul of ourselves in the spirit of everything else, we can remind ourselves whenever we want.

Contemplating Meditation

> *All man's problems*
> *lay in his inability to sit alone quietly in a room.*
> — Blaise Pascal

Fitness gurus can be dangerously straight and narrow. Nutritional experts can be downright nutty and it's not uncommon for meditation masters to look a little alien. How and why we engage in these practices determines their true value and ultimate benefit. To the extent healthy practices engender our honest attention, we've honored them in the spirit intended.

The word meditate comes from *contemplate*. Contemplate means *templum* or inner temple—a temple being a sacred open space. Somewhere out there between your thoughts and your things, kitty corner from time and space, there's another path to yet another dimension here in the enlightened zone.

Attention returning, slowly revolving
Around any one object, thoughts of things slowly fade black.
Lessened distraction allows now and then traction,
the moment's release.
Contemplating this copy—imagined inside—
the image is out there.
As written words collapse into reading,
A lost sense of self awakens as the essence of Self
And forever endures.

With nothing to do,
Know the ultimate intention of your own self-fulfilling Self
To relax in your resonating nature as pure purpose.

With nothing to relate to,
Relate to the absolute attention of your own self-receptive Self,
Heartily accepted by your wholly accepting nature as pure love.

With nothing to respond to,
Reply as the self-referring power of your own unreserved Self
And recall your potent nature as pure responsiveness.

With nothing holding you down,
Fly with the infinite pleasure of your own sovereign Self-rule
And witness your possible nature as pure freedom.

When fully awakened in restful awareness,
Know full well your pure loving presence
That honors your own healing prescience.
Then take control of your own *air* apparent as it honestly dawns
The reality of merely knowing and being yourself.

In a brilliant act of *at-one-ment*
All fear is forgiven, all doubt is redeemed,
All hope is enacted, and all faith is known.
Out on a limb, this risk is worth taking,
It's a near life experience that tells the big picture,
Gives the full story and deciphers the meaning.

Your willingness to live and your passion to learn
Deliver the fancy fruits of this labor of love.
Preceding yourself in spite of your self in the midst of your Self,
A purifying mind cleanses the body
to synchronize brainwaves and harmonize both.
The power and pleasure of honest attention
aligns all cells and all systems
With their natural need to be part of a team,
where simple awareness simply integrates all.

It's no big surprise that beyond
any big thoughts and any big things
Lies the meaning of purpose with love that's responsive and free.
Gradually, militant extremists bend
into mindful environ-mentalists,
Health nuts morph into fruitful health advocates,
So that fitness fanatics can stop fanning the antics.

> Now you're part of the solution instead of the problem,
> And the ambience in your home adds to the cultural tone.
> Love and will inside become willing love outside.
> Inner belonging eases most outer longing,
> Shows of strength politely bow to a subtler stamina.
> Sooner or later, aloneness is eased by *all-one-ness*
> And meaning becomes more rather than less.

The ensuing equanimity extends a levelheaded even-handedness that appreciates well-balanced values. Beneath overbearing and darkened confusion lie the underpinnings of enlightened reason. Embellished despair for momentary disaster and hysterical thrill for personal fortune is now tempered with a considerate empathy for distant cries and the extraordinary joy at life's simple pleasures.

Being equal to the occasion squares the highs with the lows and the ups with the downs. A private stability in the midst of global instability symbolizes a personal certainty in spite of utter uncertainty. It's a sensational homecoming for the homeless soul at the heart of emotional pains and aggravated assaults.

When you know in your heart and feel in your soul the meaning of health, then all that you do is naturally done with healing in mind. Now your endearing presence serves to remind all doctored souls of their own subtle essence so they too can flourish in this spiritual experience of a lifetime.

* * *

Suggested Reading

Becker, Robert O. *The Body Electric.*
Chopra, Deepak. *Ageless Body, Timeless Mind.*
Dossey, Larry. *Meaning and Medicine.*
Frankl, Viktor. *Man's Search for Meaning.*
Greenwood, Michael. *Paradox and Healing.*
Keen, Sam. *To Love and be Loved.*
Levoy, Gregg. *Callings – Finding and Following an Authentic Life.*
Lipton, Bruce. *Nature, Nurture and the Power of Love - video*
Moore, Thomas. *Care of the Soul.*
Moss, Richard. *The Second Miracle.*
Orloff, Judith. *Second Sight.*
Ornish, Dean. *Love and Survival.*
Pearce, Joseph, Chilton. *Evolution's End.*
Peck, Scott. *The Road Less Traveled.*
Ring, Kenneth. *Heading Towards Omega.*
Rinpoche, Sogyal. *The Tibetan Book of Living and Dying.*
Roberts, Jane. *The Nature of the Psyche, The Nature of Personal Reality.*
Sheldrake, Rupert. *Seven Experiments That Could Change The World.*
Siegel, Bernie. *Peace, Love, and Healing.*
Suzuki, David. *The Sacred Balance: Rediscovering Our Place in Nature.*
Swimme, Brian. *The Universe Story.*
Welwood, John. *Love and Awakening.*
Wilber, Ken. *A Brief History of Everything, Up From Eden/Atman Project.*
Yogi, Maharishi Mahesh. *The Science of Life and the Art of Living.*

Gary Ratson, MD
Vancouver, BC Canada
the_souldoc@hotmail.com

Gary Ratson is a Canadian physician who graduated from medicine at the University of Manitoba in 1986 with an undergraduate degree in chemistry. He began his career in sports medicine in Halifax at the Fenwick Sport Medicine and Orthopedic Clinic of Nova Scotia. Throughout the ensuing decade, he studied many ancient healing traditions and practices including Ayurvedic medicine, acupuncture, hypnosis, meditation, and yoga.

The Meaning of Health—the Experience of a Lifetime began as a poem that expressed his core insights about physical, emotional, and spiritual health. It gradually grew into a seminar for the support groups around Winnipeg and then naturally evolved into its present form. By the time each chapter was a bulky thirty or forty pages, Gary decided to set out on the high seas for some final inspiration with other doctors who were sailing around the world.

The conditions sailing across the Pacific Ocean were less than conducive for any heavy duty writing or deep thinking. Reading novels was about the best anybody aboard could muster. But the yearlong adventure was indeed the experience of a lifetime. Gary seemed to find his writing voice somewhere in the many humorous novels aboard *Stitches Explorer* and in the wild adventures waiting on the islands.

Disembarking on the island of Bali in Indonesia, Gary spent the next two months in Sanur whittling his rather wooden tome down to a livelier read. All the while, he tried to block out the wild roosters, screaming monkeys, traditional Balinese drumming rituals, and millions of scooters. Back in Vancouver and over the next six months, the final rewriting and rewriting culminated in what amounts to his life's work—thus far.

ISBN 141200228-1